le Dossier

of Hortense de Monplaisir

le Dossier

of Hortense de Monplaisir

or

How to Survive the English

Translated by Sarah Long

JOHN MURRAY

First published in Great Britain in 2007 by John Murray (Publishers)
An Hachette Livre UK company

2

A CIP catalogue record for this title is available from the British Library

ISBN 978-0-7195-6846-6

Typeset in Monotype Sabon by Servis Filmsetting Ltd, Manchester

Printed and bound by Clays Ltd, St Ives plc

John Murray policy is to use papers that are natural, renewable and
recyclable products and made from wood grown in sustainable forests. The
logging and manufacturing processes are expected to conform to the
environmental regulations of the country of origin.

John Murray (Publishers)
338 Euston Road
London NW1 3BH

www.johnmurray.co.uk

About the author

Hortense de Monplaisir is from a very old French family who did not need to buy their *particule*. After studying at Sciences Po*, she married a *grosse légume* in banking and has made a career embellishing his grey world with her vivacious conversation and colourful table displays. Thanks to her expatriation, her children are bilingual and *au fait* with binge drinking culture, whilst preferring to sip Orangina and dance *le rock* taught by a *maître-danseur* from Paris. She and her husband live in London, but have homes on Paris's Left Bank and in the Luberon, as well as one-tenth of the family *manoir* in Brittany. An incisive observer of the English, she remains French through and through. Her interests include *le scrapbooking*, painting on porcelain and organizing holidays in Verbier, St Barts and the Ile de Ré. She has an exceptional IQ and is a member of French Mensa.

About the translator

Sarah Long is the author of two novels, *And What Do You Do?* and *The Next Best Thing*. She lived in

*Translator's note: Sciences Po is one of the *grandes écoles*, or top universities.

Paris for ten years, where she met Hortense at a wine-tasting, leading to a lifelong friendship of such intensity that she paraphrases Flaubert in claiming, '*Madame de Monplaisir, c'est moi!*'

CONTENTS

le Dossier

PREFACE TO THE BRITISH EDITION

I wrote this book for my French compatriots. To help them adjust to the shock of moving to England. To lead them to understand the barbarity – and richness – of life on this peculiar little island.

Then something strange happened. My English friends were so impressed by my insights that they, too, wanted to read my book. In a fit of *nombrilisme**, they have become obsessed by their national identity! Suddenly all they think about is what it means to be English, or British, or subjects of the United Kingdom[†] – they can't even decide what they are called!

I realized then how I might come to their aid. Like Stendahl, I would hold up the mirror and let them see themselves! I arranged for my *petit guide* to be made available in their mother tongue.

So read on, my dear English friends, I dedicate this book to you!

H de M

---

*Translator's note: a widely used French word meaning navel-gazing or self-centredness.

FOREWORD: MY MISSION TO YOU

'What is England? A French colony that
didn't work out.'
Georges Clemenceau

Let me tell you how I came to write this book. It seems like only yesterday that my husband delivered the bombshell. We were taking an *apéritif* on our *balcon*, looking down on a perfect Paris spring evening. I was wearing a new top from Vanessa Bruno and looking forward to being admired in La Petite Cour, the best terrace in Paris where we had reserved a table next to the fountain. Hortense, he said, I have some good news. I have been offered a promotion which I am not about to refuse. I was not surprised. I chose my husband carefully, and it was no coincidence that he was a graduate of ENA*. I raised my glass in congratulations; he seemed almost

*Translator's note: the Ecole Nationale d'Administration, the *ne plus ultra* of elite universities.

handsome to me at that moment, with his neat grey hair and primrose yellow jacket. He smiled at me nervously. There is a *petite complication*, he said. It means transferring to head office. The job is in London.

Now, please don't misunderstand me. Like every sophisticated Parisienne, *j'adore Londres*! A little weekend escapade, *un peu de shopping*, a walk in Hyde Park through the rain, even a small glass of beer in those famous pubs, nothing could be more refreshing. And on the way back in Eurostar, pots of Whittard's tea in our Dior bags, how we loved to laugh about the eccentricities of the English, safe in the knowledge that we were returning to the centre of the civilized world. But to install ourselves there full time? *Tu exagères*!

You will see, my husband said, it is a marvellous opportunity for you. You will be an *ambassadrice* for French *savoir-faire*. You will shine in the salons of South Kensington. You will walk tall and elegant amongst those lumpen English women. And fiscally, it is very interesting.

Three months later, I found myself mistress of a *chérissime* doll's house off Fulham Road, barely large enough to contain my wardrobe. When the removal van had left, my husband said, let us go for dinner. There is a famous *crêperie* on the King's Road.

(We love *crêpes*, as we have kept in touch with simple pleasures.) As lumpen doughy pancakes were brought to the table with a pitiful garnish of anaemic lettuce and flavourless tomatoes, I am not ashamed to say, I wept. Huddled in my thin jacket, so inadequate against the unseasonal cold (naturally, it had been 25 degrees that morning in Paris), I gazed out at the rain and said, I cannot do this. My husband held my hand and looked quite wretched.

And then, it struck me. My exile would not be in vain. There was a reason why Hortense de Monplaisir (I preferred to keep my maiden name, those with a *particule* do not relinquish it easily) had been sent amongst the Anglo-Saxons*. I would discover and conquer London. Casanova said 'One lives in Paris, elsewhere one simply vegetates,' but I would prove him wrong. I would use my unique French sensibility to show how London can become the golden setting for the dazzling jewel that is the *Parisienne*.

Ten years on, I have achieved that goal. I have become so entirely *bi-culturelle* that I understand the English better than they do themselves. And – *noblesse oblige* – I am ready to share my observations with you.

*Translator's note: 'Anglo-Saxon' is widely used by the French to disparage all white English-speaking nations, but especially the English.

Take my hand and I will lead you through these pages to show you how it is to live in the land of the sandwich, where the men don't look at you. Where they never say what they think and laugh like hyenas at things that aren't funny. I will take you to the end of Brighton pier, introduce you to the incomprehensible Christmas pantomime and the medieval horror of the hospital waiting room. I will invite you into an Englishman's boudoir, pausing only to look at his wardrobe (*ma chère, quelle catastrophe!*) before examining the origins of his repressed sexuality. Draw up a chair, I'll pop the kettle on and we'll have a nice cup of tea while I unveil to you the mysterious ways of the English!

H de M

BEFORE WE BEGIN . . .

'How I hate the French.'

*Evelyn Waugh**

I once asked an English friend why the English were so horrid about the French. Was it because they were jealous? Oh no, he said, we don't do jealousy. It's more . . . pity.

Oh really, I said. Is that why you all want to come to live in our country, because you feel **sorry** for us?

Now, I am no psychologist, but it is evident to me that the anti-French nonsense that fills the British press is nothing more than envy. They envy us our culture, our food, our small bottoms and our ability to say *non* to anything that threatens these, be it immigrants, globalization or the importing of nasty British meat.

*In a letter to Nancy Mitford, concerning the legendary beauty Louise de Vilmorin best known to the English for seducing both Duff and Diana Cooper.

This envy is so strong that one in five of them wishes they *were* French.* I see it in their eyes when they talk to me, admiring the inimitable twist of my silk scarf. I see it in the queues of Citroëns and Renaults slavishly lined up at the ferry terminals to embark upon another fantasy trip to our proud republic. I see it in the crates of wine and oozing cheese they carry back home to tide them over until their next mini-break. I feel their pain, the *cri du coeur* that reaches out to me and shouts 'If only I were French! *Au fait* with philosophy! *Insouciant!* Engaged in a *Jules et Jim* style *ménage à trois!*'

Switch on the television and you'll see they can't get enough of us. Documentaries† show Londoners happily fleeing their homeland to hide away in some godforsaken corner of *La France profonde*.** Can you imagine a Parisian family abandoning their apartment to begin a new life in a cottage in Wales?

As a French person in England, you must embrace the flattery of this attention, and take the insults for

---

*According to a 2006 survey, indignantly reported across the national press.

†The British complain about immigration to their own country, but never stop to consider about how we might feel about them crashing their way into ours!

**Translator's note: sniffy Parisian term for any part of France that isn't Paris.

what they are: cries for help. Hopelessly in thrall to our superiority, they lash out like inarticulate children. I was in a café in South Kensington with a friend who was bemoaning the frustrations of London life. Suddenly a red-faced man at the next table leaned across.

'If you don't like it,' he shouted, pointing to the door, 'Cromwell Road, turn left, Heathrow, aeroplane, go home, *au revoir*!'

I am happy to say I acquitted myself most elegantly. 'My good man,' I said, 'I love this city, and have many English friends, who have the manners you so evidently lack.'

The entire café abandoned the traditional British reserve and broke out in spontaneous applause. It was another small victory for France.

How to Spot an Englishwoman

'English Women: be amazed they have such pretty
children.'

Gustave Flaubert, Dictionary of Commonplaces

* * *

'Most of them have ugly faces.'

Odette Keun,* I Discover the English

When I first learned of our move to England,
I went round to tell my dearest *copine* Marie-
Chantal. We were giving up smoking together, and
were engaged in a therapy involving massage and the
spraying of *eau cellulaire*, and I admit I was feeling
very emotional. How would I cope, I said, how could
I bear to be torn away from my weekly *brushing* with
my coiffeur *fétiche* and everything I so adored about
my darling Paris, to be banished to the land of sensible shoes and pot-bellied women?

---

*Mistress of English writer H. G. Wells, embittered by his
refusal to marry her.

Look on the bright side, she said. At least you won't have to worry about Pierre-Marie cheating on you.

Now, I don't want to be unfair. Many British women are great beauties. Charlotte Rampling, Kristin Scott Thomas and Jane Birkin, for instance, although of course they live in France. But there may be a grain of truth in the old French joke: What do you call a beautiful woman in London? Answer: a tourist!

Big faces, pear-shaped torsos with heavy low-slung bosoms . . . one could be cruel about the English physique, and Odette Keun did not mince her words: 'She is badly jointed and cannot handle herself properly; there is something in the cut of her body and the swing of her limbs that makes her more awkward and less alluring than her European sister – she really walks horribly, and her feet are huge.'

At least they've caught on to orthodentistry now and you don't see so many 'teeth that chase the steak', to use a French expression. But to my practised eye – and I have had ten years to make this judgement – there is nothing wrong with the raw material, it's just that they don't know how to showcase their charms. They may buy fashion magazines, go on endless diets, rush round clothes shops in a buying frenzy, but 'at the end of the day' (as they like to say) English-women are just not that bothered what they look like, and take the heretical view that appearances don't matter! For them, it's just a game, whereas for us, it is a matter of life and death.

The British press takes great pleasure in women failing to look good. Whole pages are devoted to photographs of celebrities getting it wrong: heavy bosoms falling out of cocktail dresses, pixie boots, helmet hair, ill-judged accessories.

In France we could never run such pages, even if we wanted to. Why? Because you could never find women in the the public eye looking embarrassing. Remember that shot of Ségolène Royale in her bikini? A political leader in her fifties with the body of a twenty-five-year-old. It made me so proud to be French.

Introducing 'Bee'

Many of my insights into the English have been inspired by my next-door neighbour. Her real name is Beatrice, 'But call me Bee,' she said when we met for the first time, in that over-familiar way the English have of forcing nicknames upon total strangers. She came crashing into my life the day we moved into our London house. Pierre-Marie was directing the removal men and I was lying down upstairs with a migraine, when she appeared at the bedroom door with an enormous mug of tea and a plate of short-bread. 'This will perk you up,' she said, and wouldn't leave until I had eaten it, even though I never take *goûter*.

A cheerful size 14 (42 for those of you not yet *au fait* with the archaic measures here), she encapsulates the essence of *le style anglais*. On a good day, I would say eccentric. On a bad day, I would say *en pagaille*. Having seen her outfits evolve – or should that be, lurch wildly – over ten years, I can say that I have a good appreciation of the rules of English dress sense, which I am ready to share with you here:

How to dress like an Englishwoman

CHEAP AND CHEERFUL
Coco Chanel said 'Fashion fades, only style remains the same.' Which is why we Frenchwomen prefer to invest in classic pieces that will still look stunning in ten years' time (we are also confident they will still fit us in ten years' time).

Perhaps because their weight fluctuates according to their yo-yo dieting patterns, the English prefer to go in for bulimic buying sprees. We've seen photographs of the England footballers' wives and girl-friends weighed down with designer bags at airports. Most women can't afford this, but echo the sentiment by going wild in Topshop and Primark, intoxicated by the low prices. Bee refers to Primark as 'Primarni' as a sneer at those who prefer to pay proper prices for their clothes.

JANE EYRE VS MADAME BOVARY

'You think too much about your *toilette* . . . it's the person inside that matters.' So says that dreary little governess Jane Eyre* to her French charge, Adèle. Drab role model for every schoolgirl – and English heroine *par excellence* – plain Jane resists Mr Rochester's gallant attempts to buy her new clothes because she doesn't want to look like 'an ape in a harlequin's jacket'. What an extraordinary reaction to a suggestion that she make the best of herself!

How unlike our own Madame Bovary, whose head is turned by the sight of the fine clothes at the ball. So what if things turned out badly for her; at least she looked good.

A WOEFUL LACK OF CONFIDENCE

The touching thing about Englishwomen trying to dress is that they start from such a low base. In the

---

*Charlotte Brontë's *Jane Eyre* is every Englishwoman's favourite novel, an improbable rags-to-riches tale in which goodness and determination prevail over beauty.

humiliating television show *What Not To Wear*, women are stripped to their underwear and forced to look at their bodies in the mirror, often, it appears, for the first time in their lives. They usually weep. They are then helped into buying clothes that suit them, as though they were children instead of sturdy matrons. Can you imagine such a show in France?

MUTTON DRESSED AS LAMB

A sorry side-effect of Topshop is women dressing inappropriately to their age. Flouncy mini-skirts may be cheap and 'fun' but that's exactly why they should be left to our daughters, as should low-cut jeans revealing pale tyres of flesh. Bee got rather annoyed with me when I said this, and started muttering about 'old French lizards'. She then slipped back into her default green quilted jacket and blowsy floral dress which she always wears when she's feeling depressed and imagination fails her.

NOTHING MUST MATCH

'That will do' is the thinking here behind trying to match accessories.

'Oh, you French, you're just too neat!' was Bee's retort when I pointed out that the red of her scarf was several clashing shades off the burgundy of her skirt. Bee thinks it is 'middle-aged' to be what she calls over-coordinated, but as I tried to explain to her, it's a question of harmony.

WEAR TRAINERS

We wear trainers for sport, and if we want something simple and flat for town wear, then ballerinas are the answer. The English wear trainers everywhere. I prefer to wear heels, for the same reason as I like to wear a *bustier* – it forces me to have good posture.

BODEN

The best short cut to the English look can be found in the 'jolly hockey sticks' Boden mail order catalogue. Large pale Englishmen are photographed in the country, cavorting with 'good sport' girlfriends, with captions from Johnnie Boden himself that assume the reader has no knowledge or feeling for clothes. He wears high-waisted cords described as 'sturdy perennials', while she downs a pint of bitter in a lurid floral cardigan and a camisole 'cut to conceal, not to reveal'. Boden is hugely popular with middle classes trapped in London terraced houses who dream of 'moving out' to achieve a Charles and Camilla lifestyle.

Flicking through the catalogue always makes me feel rather low and sets me pining for the Boulevard Saint-Germain, particularly when I read Johnnie's copy for an unusually drab A-line box-pleated skirt:

'I can imagine you catching sight of this in your wardrobe on a grey Monday and breaking into an irrepressible smile.' I don't think so.

LINGERIE

Bee thinks it's not worth spending money on underwear, as nobody sees it (I assume she means her husband when she says nobody). I would say that no woman can afford to pass up the opportunity to feel *éclatante et séduisante*; and when in Paris, I always buy a little something at Fifi Chachnil on the rue St-Honoré.

Lots of English girls favour the *stripteaseuse* look. Just take a look at the fluorescent waspies and crazy *strings* on sale at the cheap high street chains, and you'll see what I mean. *Pas très classé.*

Most Englishwomen buy their lingerie in Marks & Spencer, as it can be scooped into a wire basket along with the ready meals and tried on in the privacy of their bedroom, where nobody will tell them that it doesn't fit. But the single bestselling bra in England is made by Triumph and called Doreen. It comes in sizes up to 60DD, which is off the scale for conversion to French, and is endorsed by one grateful customer as follows:

'When I drove over speed bumps, I knew I had the right bra. Usually I bounce all over the place.'

HAIR

Hair must be messy; they don't care for a neat French bob or a chignon. This is in the keeping with the Bohemian look the English achieve quite well with clothes from Jigsaw or Monsoon. I have known a number of rather *coincé* Frenchwomen who have abandoned the *très correct* hairbands and Catholic bourgeois Cyrillus separates for a more flowing look, which is not altogether a bad thing. Let travel broaden our minds!

MAKE-UP

Usually Bee wears no make-up at all. Fortunately for her she has good English skin, well nourished by her physique. But when she goes out in the evening, it's all guns blazing, with eyes, lips and cheeks aglow. I can't help thinking of Bernard Henri Lévy's remark that he could never fall in love with a woman in power, because her make-up is badly applied.*

DRESS DOWN

In France it is a form of disrespect to wear a tracksuit and flipflops to the post office, and we would never go out to buy the bread without looking *habillée*. Believe me, the English have no such scruples. Some

*In his book *Men and Women*, co-written with Françoise Giroud.

Frenchwomen find it liberating to live in England where nobody cares what they are wearing, but personally I find it depressing.

How to Spot an Englishman

My neighbour Bee has unkind and unjustified things to say about Pierre-Marie's dress sense. When we invited her round for an informal summer barbecue, she made much of his primrose cashmere sweater thrown around his shoulders, and his pointed shoes that she found 'dodgy'. 'I love it,' she said, shrieking with laughter (she had clearly already taken several aperitifs), 'you Frenchmen, you crack me up!'

Needless to say, there were plenty of other Frenchmen present, mostly with pastel sweaters around the shoulders, though as I said to Beatrice, if she could think of a more appropriate way to dress for a changeable British summer evening, I would be pleased to hear it. Nor did I see that a sensitivity to colour and fine Italian leather is in any way a sign of homosexuality, which was her theme later in the evening, when all the other guests had left. It was *un peu exagéré*, I thought, coming from the wife of an Englishman.

So, in swift revenge, here is my checklist for Englishmen:

THE ENGLISH LOOK

- Ginger hair and mottled pink-white complexion

- Large beige trousers to house thighs like tree-trunks

- Striped shirt with ginger fuzz sticking out of it

- Chunky lace-up shoes – never pointy or slip-on which might mark him out as 'dodgy'

- 'Beef and pudding face' which the 18th century travel guide writer Thicknesse pointed out would look silly under a dainty French hat

- Sandals worn with socks

CROSS-DRESSING: A VERY ENGLISH PASSION

I cannot write about Englishmen without mentioning their fondness for dressing up as ladies. It starts at their single-sex schools, where boys have to play female roles in all-male theatrical productions. They often wear dresses that are too short, hovering several centimetres above their big schoolboy shoes.

Later on, as burly university students, they will collect money for 'rag week' in full make-up and crinoline.

May I refer once more to Johnnie Boden's catalogue copy here, wistfully describing one of his skirts: 'I can only imagine the feel of the viscose swishing around your legs, but you get to experience it first hand. And they talk about equality of the sexes!'

A Frenchman would never write in such terms.

The obituary of a distinguished English publisher mentioned his participation at a launch party, in which a team of men dressed as Queen Victoria played hockey against another male team of Florence Nightingales on a frosty morning in Hyde Park. This could not happen in France.

Why the English Don't Care What They Look Like

I must end this chapter by offering you my personal view of why the English don't dress well. It's a Protestant thing. Vanity is despised. Appearances don't matter. Keep your eyes and your hands to yourself. Which is why, when you walk down a street in England, you might just as well be dressed like a fright, because *nobody is going to look at you*. This upset me at first. Had I lost my charms? I tried again in the company of a beautiful actress: same result. No eye contact, no simmering acknowledgement, no seduction. Eyes down, walk past, don't even go there. No sex please, we're British. Which brings me neatly to my next chapter.

2

The English and Sex

'As flat, stale and deadly as a slab of one of his own cold suet puddings. In brief: in bed, he's boring.'

Odette Keun, on the English male's sexual technique

It is well known that Englishmen are no good at sex. They go at it in a medieval fashion, blind drunk, ignorant and with no respect for *la séduction*.

Or at least that's what I thought before I came to live in England, and I have seen nothing since to make me change my mind. I was rather hoping that a dashing Englishman might sweep me off my feet and prove me wrong, but I have yet to encounter such an *aventure*, unless you count the drunken pass that Bee's husband Hereward made at me one Christmas Eve.

At risk of sounding *prétentieuse*, I would say the act of love for the French is a Renaissance sculpture. For the English, it is a Lucien Freud painting, or a dirty seaside postcard. They'd rather be down the pub, at the match or in the garden shed.

The only Englishman who is any good at sex is the pop singer Sting, who once mentioned his fondness for eastern methods of lovemaking. If you mention his name to an Englishman, he will say 'Tantric sex' with a snort of derision at the idea of wanting to linger over the act instead of getting it over as soon as possible.

To attract male attention, Englishwomen have to go out 'on the pull' dressed like tarts. Thankfully, my own son has declared them *sans grace* and vowed to marry a French girl who knows the meaning of elegant restraint.

When the English do 'score' (sporting vocabulary is *de rigueur* for sex), the rules are clear. In no way must the sex ever be discussed, although it might be conceded that last night was 'a laugh'.

Altogether, it is a mystery how they ever procreate.

Let us examine some of the sexual eccentricities of our poor neighbours, in an attempt to understand why they fall so short of our own high standards in the art of love.

Only When Drunk

My dear friend Marie-Cha tells me an illuminating tale about her time at an English university. A demure girl, buttoned up in Liberty-print dress and Alice band, came to borrow a book from Marie-Cha's room. She shyly greeted Marie-Cha's father who pronounced her a thoroughly suitable friend. So sweet, so British, it was clear butter wouldn't melt in her mouth! Yet this girl was the most sexually liberated person Marie-Cha had ever met. Like many English girls, she would go out, drink herself to oblivion, perform lewd acts of Boschian intensity, *but only when she was drunk*. The next morning, the Alice band was back, the depravity never spoken of.

It's the same with boys: they cannot muster the courage to 'get off' with girls unless they are inebriated. I am often taken by a wave of homesickness when I see young people on a night out in London. Boys up one end of the pub drinking pints of beer, girls at the other side knocking back vodka cocktails, screeching with raucous laughter as they hurl insults from one group to the other. What a contrast to Paris, where you see civilized mixed groups of boys and girls – as nature intended! – quietly sipping an Orangina at a sedate café before going home to their parents to study. You will understand the importance of *les rallyes** that we have set up in London, to ensure our sons do not fall prey to local habits, and get to meet the right sort of French girl.

*See Chapter 16, Education.

Sex is a Dirty Joke

They might not care for sex itself, but the British appetite for sex jokes is boundless. If you have a French accent, you will be a natural target for *double entendres** and lewd winks as 'French' is shorthand for 'sex' (as in French knickers, *soixante-neuf* and Napoleon's urgent message to Josephine: 'I'm coming home – don't wash', which they find very funny).

Sex jokes are everywhere; anything that relates to the physical expression of love is treated with a furtive snigger. In England they laugh at athletes for being impressively endowed[†], give an annual 'bad sex award' for literature, and buy birthday cards with 'adult content' warnings, that show grotesque couplings between busty girls and funny little men. Where we have the erotically charged *film noir*, the English have the TV sitcom inviting viewers to 'have a laugh' at the couple sitting in bed in their pyjamas and joking about their sexual failure.

*The English use French words to allude to anything they consider sexual, eg *embonpoint*, which they mistakenly believe refers only to big breasts, not to being overweight in general.
[†]Linford Christie's 'lunchbox' was inexplicably considered amusing.

Young men's magazines with *double-entendre* names like *Loaded* or *Nuts** give a 'humorous' twist to soft porn, inviting readers to compete for a date with a woman photographed naked with a bag over her head 'because there is something wrong with her face'.

You will understand this is not a culture conducive to harmonious sexual relations.

Segregating the Sexes

In the words of Abbé le Blanc, 'Frenchmen enjoy the company of women, Englishmen fear it.'

Victorian art critic John Ruskin famously fainted on his wedding night at the sight of his wife's pubic hair. Modern Englishmen may be better informed (see 'Pornography' below), yet many of Pierre-Marie's English colleagues went through their entire adolescence without speaking to a girl. Reared in remote boarding schools, their only female contact was with Matron, which explains the erotic significance of the Nurse in books and films produced by ex-public[†] schoolboys.

---

*Humorous pun on slang word meaning crazy/the male genitalia.
[†]By public of course I mean private: see Chapter 16, Education.

Single-sex schools are slowly falling from favour, but English social life is still very much a case of 'ladies and gentlemen'. Let me talk you through some same-sex institutions that appear curious – even barbarous – to us, who cannot conceive of an agreeable evening that is not *mixte*.

• Hen Parties. Vulgar drunken evenings where the future bride and her girlfriends behave like hookers in the presence of a male stripper. Perhaps accurately, the bride assumes that her *vie amoureuse* is about to come to an end, so they are often maudlin affairs.

• Stag Parties. Typically a weekend in Amsterdam where the groom and his mates become inebriated at lap-dancing clubs and have the kind of clumsy sexual encounters they most enjoy. Pierre-Marie says the one he attended was the longest evening of his life, and he was made to feel like a *pédé* because he drank beer in half-pint 'lady' glasses.

• Gentlemen's Clubs. Institutions that continue the boarding-school ethos, so men still don't need to talk to women. They serve nursery food to old men snoozing on leather chairs and women are not admitted. When I was shown round the Garrick, on a visit with *Londres Accueil*, we were told that ladies, though barred from membership, were allowed as guests, and that rooms were available. Of course we all laughed a little, thinking this would be for the *cinq à sept*, but our guide did not understand our amusement. As far as he was concerned, the rooms were for country gentlemen to sleep in when they come up to town, and no sex has ever taken place here.

• Working Men's Clubs. Proletarian versions of gentlemen's clubs. Women not admitted.

• Women Leaving the Table. Now defunct except in highest society. An uncivilized device whereby women leave the table after the meal just as the conversation is becoming interesting. They must wait in a side room while the men drink port.

• Book Clubs. Women-only groups which discuss a book for five minutes before moving on to boast about their children's achievements and home improvements. Men are not invited.

• Anne Summers Parties. Where women buy 'naughty' lingerie in the hope of livening up their men.

• The Sex Discrimination Law Suit. In France we consider it gallant when a male colleague compliments us on our appearance, but here it can land him in court.

Le Vice anglais

The English cruel streak is given full rein in their taste for baroque forms of sexual gratification. Spanking flourished in boarding school before it became illegal, and there is still moist-eyed nostalgia for the days when one's 'fag'* dropped his short trousers to have his buttocks beaten. You regularly read details of spanking judges, etc., in the gutter press.

The English Homosexual

I am a tireless champion for human rights, so one of the things I adore about England is the tolerance accorded to minorities. I unreservedly applaud the high profile enjoyed by homosexuals, making London the gay capital of Europe. They've come a long way since Oscar Wilde had to flee to Paris!

Will you bear with me while I give you a brief history of the English homosexual?

In 1944 the booklet *Advice to British Servicemen* warned that the French were deeply shocked by music-hall jokes about 'nancy boys'. These nancy boys lie at the heart of the English sexual psyche.

---

*Slang term for young boy who performs services for older boy at boarding school.

They appear in *Carry On* films and pantomimes, and play useless husbands on TV comedy shows. Nancy boys from boarding schools grew up to become 'confirmed bachelors' who shared lodgings, like Sherlock Holmes and Dr Watson. They never had sex, rather they were loveable eccentrics who were 'just not interested in that sort of thing'. This was a very comfortable idea to the low-libido English who have made a national treasure of the camp playwright Alan Bennett and agreed with singer Boy George when he said he would rather have a cup of tea than sex.

Gay pride has now brought the nancy out of his sexless ghetto. He has laid down the feather duster to come roaring priapically into the heart of the establishment, where he networks with a vengeance. The *Independent* newspaper publishes an annual pink list of top gays in business and the arts, and I sometimes wonder if the English become gay just to enjoy the fabulous social life. It's like a modern version of the gentlemen's club: women not admitted (or at least, not noticed), vodka cocktails and salmon blinis instead of port and suet pudding, *plus ça change* . . .

Alongside the vibrant homosexual community, there are sadly still a few closeted politicians, born too late to profit from the sex revolution, who are routinely photographed 'cottaging' in London parks.

I am told there are also lesbians in England, but I've never met any. To be honest, all Englishwomen look a bit like lesbians.

My neighbour Bee, after a few drinks, once asked me what the difference was between an English and a French homosexual. 'The French homosexual is married!' she shrieked, slopping her gin down the front of her dress. She then recounted how her gay friend (all Englishwomen are intimate with homosexual men) regularly went to Paris in summer to pick up *pères de famille* in the Tuileries gardens while their wives were on the Ile de Ré with the children.

I wasn't sure if she was trying to cast doubt on my own husband. He always used to stay in Paris in July and join us for weekends. But then so did all my friends' husbands; in fact they often had dinner together, on a warm *terrasse*, a rare chance for *mec en mec* conversation, before strolling back to their deserted apartments . . . But I must hasten to reassure you that there is *nothing* lacking in the *vie intime* of our couple. And anyway, Pierre-Marie didn't go to boarding school.

'Read All About It!'

Instead of a sex life, the British have their newspapers. And I don't just mean the Page Three girls with their blank eyes and bare breasts, nor do I mean the pornography industry, even if they are the biggest European consumers of internet porn.*

No, porn is just a diverting sideline. What they really love is SCANDAL: catching people out; punishing them for daring to have sex. This is completely in keeping with the puritan tradition.

Picture the English couple in bed on Sunday morning. I am speaking here of my neighbours Bee and Hereward, but it could be any English couple. They have got the weekly sex over, thank goodness. They may even have taken off their Marks & Spencer pyjamas. They'll have had their little joke: 'Well, that's got that out of the way for another month.' Then Hereward will go down to the dungeon kitchen to make a pot of tea. On the way up, he'll pick up the papers that have been thrust through the letterbox (newspaper delivery is the only service better here than in France), and with a sigh of true happiness, they will both sink back with a cup of tea and begin the 'muck-raking' that is so very much more enjoyable than their own lacklustre lovemaking.

It's the details that fascinate. The politician's mistress who is so 'glad he kissed me', reassuring the reader that he is as useless in bed as any Englishman.

*One in four British adults downloaded pornographic images last year.

The prince's envy of his mistress's tampon, my goodness how gauche! Lady X's ex-convict husband who's ditched her for the ugly *jeune fille au pair*. The fear in the eyes of the TV presenter snapped by the paparazzi as he leaves his mistress. Every foible, tirelessly examined. This is the stuff of life, this is what makes the stolid English heart beat faster.

To which I say, to borrow a favourite English phrase, 'Get a life!' Or, more specifically, 'Get a sex life!'.

Of course, we in France know that our politicians have lovers. *Et alors?* It is bad manners to speak of it, and I find it perfectly reasonable that a magazine editor should be sacked for running photos of a politician's wife with her boyfriend. Our private life should remain our own, or all is lost.

Attitudes to Les Femmes d'un certain âge

Here is a joke I found on a birthday card, showing a cartoon couple:

WIFE: 'My personal trainer says I have the bust of a twenty-four-year-old.'

HUSBAND: 'What did he say about your fifty-year-old arse?'*

*Although this 'joke' would not work in French, as our fifty-year-old women all have *les fesses d'une femme de vingt-quatre ans*.

How sad, how disrespectful, that the sexuality of the mature woman should be so ridiculed, and I am not just saying that because I am myself in the prime of my middle years! The playwright Alan Bennett is one of many English writers who portray ladies of a certain age as battleaxes for whom sex is a hilarious rarity. In his play *The History Boys*, there is a nudge-nudge reference to someone's wife who 'will be subject to some interference herself!', while in *A Private Function*, good news is celebrated with a rare offer: 'I think sexual intercourse is in order.' How the audience laughed, and how repugnant this is to us with our respect for women whatever their age.

While Catherine Deneuve is still considered one of the most beautiful and desirable women, Dame Judi Dench is consigned to the cosy sex-free status of 'national treasure'. We wouldn't dream of insulting our actress like that. She is Catherine Deneuve, not a funny old thing to put on the mantelpiece.

They Wish They Were French

The Victorian poet Matthew Arnold spoke for all England when he attacked the lubricity of the French, and even now the English are confused and envious of our success as lovers. When presidential candidate

François Bayrou was asked which quality his wife most admired in him, he replied '*Ma virilité*': an unthinkable reply from an English politician, who is not allowed a sex life.

It is our honesty they find disturbing. Danielle Mitterand writes in her autobiography that it is hypocrisy not to expect your husband to fall in love with someone else as you get older. My English friends often ask me, wistfully, 'Is it true that most of you French have lovers?' And I always reply, 'Of course, I think we French need to have a heart that beats, a reason to get up in the morning.' This need not mean that we *really* have lovers, just that the *esprit* is there, we are constantly alive to the possibility of *un petit frisson*.

Let me end, rather naughtily, by comparing myself with an Englishwoman. I don't want to boast – we are in the land of false modesty after all! – but I have to say that, as a Frenchwoman, I am *bien dans ma peau*. Needless to say, this does not translate into English! Shall we say: comfortable, confident in my sexuality. I dress with quiet elegance, my body is lithe and trim beneath my Issey Miyake, I am ready to meet the admiring gaze of a passerby when I am in France*. I am also over forty.

*Not an option in England, as I have made clear!

The point is that Frenchwomen are alive to their sexuality, whatever their age. How unlike my poor English sisters!

Now, I have an interesting theory about English (Protestant) women. I think they put on weight after forty in order to ward off temptation. If they look heavy, they won't feel like having sex, and they won't attract the discreet admiring glances that we French (Catholic) women live for. *C'est vrai, non?*

Can I leave you with three visual snapshots, to compare French and English *allure*?

Catherine Deneuve *vs* Judi Dench
Ségolène Royale *vs* Margaret Beckett
Arielle Dombasle *vs* Jade Goody

I think I've made my point?

3

You've Got to Laugh! The English and Humour

'The English language created a word, humour,
to express a hilarity, which is in the blood almost
as much as in the mind.'

Madame de Staël

Madame de Staël was absolutely right, it was the English who invented humour. They are very, very funny!

It wasn't until I came to live in England that I realized quite how funny they are. From friendly insults: 'Carry on taking the tablets!' and car bumper stickers: 'Windsurfers do it standing up!' to witty apologies for using bad language: 'Pardon my French!', you find that jokes are what make up the fabric of *la société anglaise*.

I soon learned that the worst insult you can throw at an English person is to say he has no sense of humour. You can tell him he's stupid, mean, lazy, and he won't really mind. In fact, he'll probably agree with you.

But try telling him he's not funny, and he could get quite nasty. No one's as funny as the English, he'll insist, eyes narrowing, irony is our amniotic fluid. We're hilarious, everyone knows that.

I must admit their sense of humour is not always easy to understand. For instance, the English find the following things funny:

Taking a bottle of Fitou labelled '*Seigneur d'arse*'
    to a dinner party
Wearing a red nose
Jeering at the working class (called chavs)
Using suppositories

The English also pride themselves on being able to 'take a joke' . . . Not only do we dish it out, they say, we can also take it back. This is not always true. When Jacques Chirac made a throwaway joke about British cuisine*, there was stony-faced outrage in the English newspapers. Such a reaction from the French would have been branded 'a major sense of humour failure', but it's all right for the English to get huffy when it suits them!

---

*Chirac's whispered aside was overheard by a French journalist, who disloyally passed it on to his English *homologues*. See page 36.

As part of your 'Survive the English' guide, let me give you a quick introduction to English humour – you'll certainly need it! To paraphrase a message often printed on their office mugs, 'You don't have to be crazy to live here – but it helps!!'

GSOH

In lonely heart ads, the most widely touted quality is GSOH. This stands for Good Sense of Humour, and is the key to sexual success. Which is ridiculous, because as Milan Kundera pointed out, 'laughter kills sex'. GSOH will compensate for bad clothes, poor physique and lack of social standing.

All English people think they possess a GSOH, the way that all French people think they have good taste.

Toilet Humour

The English betray their Germanic origins in their fondness for toilet jokes. Sex is treated as an extension of the toilet function: excreting, fornicating, it's all the same, all deeply shameful and therefore a fit subject for laughter.

Then there is the room itself. Many express their GSOH by papering the walls of their lavatory with cartoons and leaving a pile of joke books on the floor.

My *correspondante*'s mother placed a model of the Rodin statue *Le Baiser* in the lavatory alcove, so she could call it the Kiss and Piss room.

Pub lavatories give full vent to the owners' GSOH. On a weekend in the country, after lunching in a rather formal restaurant annexe, I was led into the toilets to admire a huge and grotesque mural representing fat ladies with handbags queueing for . . . the toilet. Hilarious, *non*?

Finally there is a huge joke about what you call the toilet, which the English enjoy because it is about class. In case you are interested, 'toilet' is 'common', 'loo' is upper class, 'lavatory' is middle class, 'bog' is jokey and 'lav' is post-modern hip. Don't say 'bathroom', that is American and therefore despised. It makes you grateful for the egalitarian ubiquity of *les toilettes*.

Stand-up Comedians: Be Funny or Die

In France, our cleverest children study science to train as engineers and doctors. In England, the cleverest children pretend they're no good at science so they can study the arts and become stand-up comedians. So solemnly is the business of humour taken that the most a parent could ever want for their child is a standing ovation at the Edinburgh fringe festival.

Joking Apart

Listen to English people when they are judging others. 'He's OK,' one might say, but then add dismissively, 'a bit serious.'

Worse even than being a 'bit serious' in general, is being serious about oneself. 'How do you like your new boss/neighbour/doctor,' you may ask. You know there's trouble if the reply comes 'He takes himself a bit seriously'. There is no character defect *plus grave*.

How different from our own culture, where being *sérieux* is a compliment: a hardworking, knowledgeable professional, rather than a trivial time-waster. Who on earth would want a doctor, or a builder, or a friend for that matter, who was *not* serious? Only the English.

Self-deprecation

A large part of the famous English humour – allied to 'not taking yourself too seriously' – consists in undermining one's own achievements, which is very wearisome. I was sitting next to a prizewinning professor once, who told me he 'fiddled around in a lab' for a living. This false modesty is considered most amusing, and the joke is on you when you later discover he is in fact the cleverest man in the world. I call it dishonest and bad manners.

The Humour of Failure

In France, we do not think that failure is a laughing matter, but the English find it hilarious. The hapless lovers in Richard Curtis films, the useless manager in *The Office*, the world's worst spy in *'Allo 'Allo*, all are loveable comedy icons.

Successful people ingratiate themselves by talking about their early failures. If an English actor is interviewed, he will laughingly recount his dismal performance in a god-forsaken provincial theatre. A business tycoon will recall being sacked for incompetence. A bestselling author will boast about how many rejection letters he received.

We prefer to keep these humiliations to ourselves.

Joke Books

In a land where a GSOH is the most valued attribute, what better gift for Christmas than a funny book? Shops have tables groaning with little 'humour' titles for the English to enjoy with their turkey, usually about toilets, failures and the French.

Jokes about the French

Still the best way to make the English laugh; they just can't leave us alone.

Like this one I heard at the theatre. 'You'd love Vienna,' says a man to a girl he is chatting up on the plane, 'it's like Paris but without the French.' Cue howls of laughter. Why is that funny? It's as if I told French audience, 'You'd love Dublin. It's like London without the English.' Nobody would laugh.

They also jeer at us for enjoying certain English comedians they now consider unfashionable, like the wonderful Benny Hill.

But the Best is French

The English discredit us by pointing out that the word 'humour' only entered the French language in 1932, but they are missing the point. We had sophisticated subdivisions: *esprit, farce* and – most appropriate to English humour – *bouffonerie*, but too much finesse to lump such disparate elements together under one crude umbrella.

The best English humour comes from France. *Private Eye* and *Spitting Image* were shamelessly lifted from *Le Canard Enchaîné* and *Les Guignols*. *Monty Python* comes from our surrealist DaDa movement. *Carry On* films are pure Molière. We even gave them April Fool's Day.*

We French enjoy humour, but we keep it in its place. It is part of a well-balanced life, but only a part, which the English cannot understand, preferring to make a joke out of absolutely everything.

Marcel Pagnol said God gave laughter to humans as consolation for being intelligent. In France we concentrate on the intelligence, and leave the English to wallow in the consolation.

---

*France was the first European country to change the calendar in 1564 under Charles IX, making 1 January the start of the year instead of 2 April, and ridiculing those fools who still thought 1 April was New Year's Eve. We mark the occasion by sticking paper fishes on to peoples backs – *très amusant!* – but the English prefer to engage in laborious practical jokes.

4

How the English Eat

'After Finland, it's the country with the worst food.
How can you trust people who eat as badly as that?'

*Jacques Chirac**

President Chirac caused an international furore when he dared to say what every French person knows to be true: English food is rubbish.

He touched on the greatest fear of all of us who bravely abandon *la meilleure cuisine du monde* to take 'pot luck' in the land of plastic bread. How will we manage? We must either waste away, or – more frighteningly – put on fifteen kilos.

I'd like to reassure you on two counts. First, I have not put on any weight in ten years, thanks to iron self-control and a strictly French lifestyle. Second, I must admit the situation is *moins catastrophique* than it

*This candid remark was unfortunately overheard in July 2005 and may have contributed to France losing out to the UK in the Olympic bid.

was. You will survive. And don't forget, you are only two and a half hours away from Paris, so if you are possessed by *une folle envie* for oysters, there is nothing to stop you from dropping in for lunch at La Coupole! As Nicholas Sarkozy reminded us, London is a French city now* . . . and we are no further from the City of Light than our fellow provincials in Marseille and Bordeaux!

The 'Foodie' Revolution

'Foodie' does not translate into French, as it means someone who cares about food, and show me a French person who doesn't? We would just say '*citoyen*'.

The great 'foodie' enlightenment was born in the 1990s. After centuries of indifference, the English woke up to the fact that they did not have to live on a diet of grey stew and boiled cabbage.

The voluptuous prophet of this movement is TV chef Nigella Lawson, blessed with a very English figure, who excites viewers by sticking her fingers in creamy bowls of cake mix. She called her first book *How to Eat*, which gives you an idea of the level of ignorance she was addressing. Her boyish

*According to *Le Monde*, London is in fact the seventh largest French city.

simple-looking co-revolutionary, Jamie Oliver, threw in his raw sexuality with *The Naked Chef*, in an attempt to convince the British that cooking wasn't just a hobby for gay men. The third TV food star was restaurateur Gordon Ramsay, a macho ex-footballer who swears a lot. Both Oliver and Ramsay keep their pretty wives in the media spotlight, to show that they are definitely not homosexual.

In spite of their pornographic curiosity in food the British really haven't got a clue. Travel around London and you'll see their idea of lunch is ripping open a sandwich on the tube, standing by their desks, or eating something unspeakable out of a paper bag as they walk. They treat food as they treat sex – something to be grabbed guiltily and quickly before they get on with what they really care about (drinking, working, reading *heat* magazine, watching television).

Eating at Home

A dining table is not an essential feature of the English home. Instead you will find huge show-off kitchens in gleaming stainless steel, designed to look like modern restaurants. Industrial-size ovens are used to heat up ready meals which are carried through to the TV room and eaten off a tray.

'Les Takeaways'

If they haven't got the energy to heat something up, the English will order in a takeaway. When we return from a week's vacation, we can barely open our front door for the mountain of menus that have piled up on the mat. I have an image of the British family, prostrate on their sofa before their large TV screen, empty pizza boxes littered round their feet as they roar with laughter at a senseless reality show.

Naturally, this is not something I will tolerate. French culture dictates that we eat together, *en famille*, over dinner sourced and prepared with care. And here we face our biggest challenge.

How the English Shop

'The only ripe fruit in England is stewed apple.'
Le comte de Lauragais

It is almost impossible to buy ripe fruit in England. Most of it is flown halfway round the world to end up in the bland giant refrigerator where 80 percent of the English food budget is spent: the British supermarket*.

*In France it is 25 percent.

Such is the hypocrisy of the 'foodie' revolution: despite all the talk about the importance of small local suppliers, the English shop almost exclusively at these *grandes surfaces*. It doesn't matter where you are in the country, there is no variety, no sense of *terroir*. They are all exactly the same, run by men in grey suits for men with grey appetites.

My First Experience of an English Supermarket

I remember the horror of my first experience. Pushing my *caddy** into the store, I was confronted by two giant aisles of 'ready meals'. The thought occurred to me that I could load up local style, with boxes of curry, Chinese and lasagne, topped up with trifle, treacle tart, mince pies, Boasters, and within a week, I could become English. For a mad moment, the idea utterly seduced me

Then I pulled myself together. Was I not an *ambassadrice* for French values? Would I allow my family to develop the slovenly habits and slack stomach of the Londoner? The coarse physique that in France we may find in the provinces, but never in Paris? I pushed my *caddy* on, towards the fruit and vegetable racks. My dears, *quelle catastrophe*! Coarse *haricots verts*

*Translator's note: *caddy* is a trolley, or a basket on wheels. It has nothing to do with golf.

shrinkwrapped in plastic, pale tomatoes, sad lettuces. As if to compensate for the poor quality, promotions urged me to take 3 for the price of 2! Tears in my eyes, I passed shelves of rubber cheese, dull-eyed fish and bags of industrial sliced bread begging to be made into soggy sandwiches. Was it for this, I thought, that I had left my beloved Saint-Germain-des-Prés?

I loaded up with Badoit, Evian and cleaning products, vowing to shop for food elsewhere, and passed to the checkout. It's for delivery, I said: of course I was not going to heave all that into my car.

'Sorry love,' she said, 'we don't do deliveries. We can get you a taxi if you want.'

I walked away from my loaded trolley and have never returned.

Since then, I have discovered there is only way to shop at a London supermarket. Order online at www.ocado.com and an agreeable man in uniform will bring you Waitrose products right into your kitchen. It's almost as good as the service I used to get in rue de l'Odeon from Ahmed at my local *arabe*.

Hunting out the Small Shops

The best small food shops are in the areas where French people live. So in west London, you can still hope to find a greengrocer *tout simple*, as opposed to the 'corner shop' where fresh food comes a poor second to newspapers, sweets and lottery tickets. Be warned that essential basic vegetables like leeks, radishes, artichokes, *feuille de chêne* and *endives* are treated as exotic rarities here, liable to be individually wrapped and sold at luxury prices.

When you do find a reasonable butcher or fishmonger, you will have to put up with Saturday morning queues of self-satisfied people nodding at each other. They will be more interested in where the meat comes from than in how it tastes.

Farmer's Markets

'Farmer's markets' are the snob end of English food retail, where *les bourgeois* make a huge fuss about thin pickings of cheese, meats and vegetables. Here you'll find the quality products we sell at every 'normal' market in France, but with less variety and at outrageous prices. Caring about food in England is a rich man's game, and makes you part of an elite club. How unlike our own democracy, where artisans and workers and *les professions libérales* stand shoulder to shoulder at the *marché,* a brotherhood of man united in their passion for food that is affordable to all.

As the name suggests, 'farmer's markets' betray a yearning for rural life, the need to dress up shopping as an agricultural experience (though where do they think vegetables come from, if not a farm? A factory?). The customers wander round like children in a theme park. Look at that dirty beetroot! Fancy that goat's cheese being rolled in paprika! Ooh look, he presses his own apples! Then they spend eighty pounds on a wild boar pâté, a few tomatoes and a bit of organic ostrich meat in plastic shrinkwrap. There is not the expertise we would expect, and if you asked a stallholder to give you a melon suitably ripe for eating tomorrow at midday, he would not be able to oblige.

The most determined 'foodie' Londoners travel miles across town to shop at the flagship Borough Market, so they can brag about it at their dinner parties. Last time I went there, I spent £53 on a small piece of salmon.

'Farmer's markets' must not be confused with traditional regular street markets which sell fruit and vegetables of varying quality at cheaper prices than you find in the supermarkets. I adore these markets: the traditional street-market trader is old-fashioned working class, complete with cockney accent and non-stop jokey patter. He might offer you an extra couple of apples 'because you've been a good girl', but is also likely to drop in a few mouldy ones.

The English won't take a *caddy* (basket on wheels) to the market because they think it makes you look old, if you are a woman, or gay, if you are a man. Instead, they prefer to stagger home with heavy bags of produce. I occasionally see an old lady with a caddy, but if you see a man pulling one, he'll be French.

French Markets

I sometimes go to the seasonal 'French markets' just to look at the British Francophile, with his wicker basket, insisting in speaking French to the stallholders, telling them about his house in the Dordogne, as if they care.

I have established a rapport with a number of *marchands* who run stalls at these events, and they make a point of keeping back something a little special for me: some *reine-claudes,* perhaps, at the point when they are just so, or some particularly fine *cèpes* in autumn. They know they cannot fool me with out-of-season food – English customers may be happy to buy peaches in February, but we know better. And as for unpasteurized cheese, who cares if camembert *au lait cru* is now illegal? For a treasured customer, there will also be something put aside inside the van, the subject of some discreet negotiation, which never fails to impress my dinner guests. But Hortense, they say, where did you find it? They know I will not tell them, as a clever shopper will never disclose her sources.

Bread

The greatest single achievement of the French colonization of London is the introduction – at least in the best areas – of the *baguette*. I buy mine in Paul, opposite South Kensington tube, but see also Bagatelle, or Maison Blanc.

Supermarkets now all sell *baguettes*. They are variously identified as 'Organic', 'Taste the difference', 'French flute', 'French stick', but none of them are any good. I prefer to stick to the *pain Poilane* that Waitrose now stock, or the heavy wholemeal loaves that are not bread as we know it, but at least preferable to an ersatz *baguette*.

To experience the full horror of British bread, I urge you to visit a Greggs bakery. Flaccid loaves, unspeakable pale cakes smothered in fluorescent icing. Pity the poor Londoners: before the invasion of the French bakers, this is what they had to put up with. People serving in baker's shops wear plastic hygienic gloves, as if to distance themselves from the unpleasantness of the product. This is what we would classify as *pâtisserie industrielle* and sell in hard-discount hypermarkets, but the English think it deserves a shop all to itself.

English Hospitality

If you are invited round for 'a drink', be warned it will be just that. Or rather, it will be 'several drinks', but nothing to eat except a few crisps. This would be all right if the occasion respected the boundaries of *l'apéritif*, but the evening is likely to lurch on well beyond dinnertime, until people either pass out, or order in a Chinese.

If you are invited to dinner, you can at least hope for something more substantial than my first experience of English hospitality. As a child, I went to stay with my aunt by marriage, who produced Ritz crackers spread with Marmite, followed by a can of Heinz tomato soup. I declined the soup, preferring to wait for the main *plat,* until my father whispered in my ear that I'd better take the soup as there was nothing to follow.

When the foodie revolution came, the English fell in love with the idea of themselves as extrovert Italians, and rushed out to buy huge pans in which to cook pasta. You are very likely to be served Italian peasant-style food, usually involving pancetta. Sometimes they get more ambitious, and become *trop stressés* as they fiddle around with quail and pomegranate on the giant steel range, bent over a stained recipe book in full view of their guests. Suddenly the 'eat-in kitchen' doesn't seem such a good idea.

On more than one occasion, I have tried to explain to my frazzled hosts that French *art de vivre* does not mean suffering in the kitchen, in fact it doesn't even mean you have to cook. There is artistry, too, in identifying the best *marchand de fromages*, in buying a *petit salé aux lentilles* from a reliable traîteur. Nobody would dream of cooking a dessert when you can buy a *tarte* from a *pâtisserie*.

When they hear this, English foodies look entirely betrayed. 'You mean, you don't cook? But you're French.'

To which I reply, 'Of course I cook, but only if I feel like it.'

My neighbour Bee has at times been less than complimentary about French home cuisine. She maintains that our national dish is a packet of frankfurters and a packet of instant mashed potato, or else a chilled roll of ready-made pastry hastily dropped into a tin and topped with beaten eggs to form a quiche. But as I say to her, there is no need to confuse the occasional *casse-croûte* improvised lunch with the carefully composed culinary habits that are the basis of our everyday life. The reason I am still the same weight as on my wedding day is that my eating patterns have remained unchanged, just adapted over the years, like a good Chanel suit. She said, ' French food, French clothes, same old boring stuff, year in, year out.' *La méchante!*

Some Abominations That Still Remain

For all their *nouveau* this, fiddly bits of that and shelves of unread glossy cookbooks, there still remain some spectacular English specialities that bring to mind one word: *immangeable* (though the word 'inedible' is rarely used here). Rest assured, you will still find the following old favourites:

Jam served with meat
Mince pies
Jelly
'Chocolate' with 30 percent cocoa content
Cheese with bits of crystallized ginger/apricot
    trapped in it.
Pepperoni
Marmite

Then there is the stuff we love, but which we fear will kill us:

'Heart attack' bacon and egg breakfasts
Clotted cream teas
Treacle tart
Fish and chips – *j'adore*!!
Les 'crème eggs' (Cadbury's)

We must fear for the globalization of English food abominations. Tesco supermarkets have now opened in China, where they sell mint jelly, sage-and-onion stuffing and Brown Sauce!

School Lunches

I have some brave friends who have chosen to send their children to their local English school. Lunch is a starvation ration of a single sandwich. The poor children are ravenous! It explains why the English school day finishes at 3.30 p.m. instead of the later continental time of 4.30: it is so the children can rush home to gorge from the snack cupboard.

By all accounts, the sandwich is preferable to the hot lunch option of deep-fried processed meat fat with chips. Shamed into action by TV chef Jamie Oliver, the government took action to implement healthier school meals. The result? The children went on hunger strike until their mothers came up to the school gates to poke junk food through the railings for them.

English children's ignorance of food is quite staggering, many of those featured on Oliver's TV programme unable to identify basic vegetables. My friend's daughter puzzled her classmates when she described a roast chicken in a lesson. They had never seen a roast chicken; for them, it was something that came in slices out of a flat plastic pack.

They should adopt our own educational initiative, *la semaine du goût,* where we instruct children on the different tastes. Though this might be over-ambitious for those who have never seen, let alone tasted a leek.

Eating Out

'The destiny of nations depends on the manner in which they feed themselves.' *Brillat-Savarin, The Physiology of Taste*

There is a modern myth that today you eat better in London than Paris. This naughty piece of propaganda is an Anglo-American conspiracy. They talk about 'variety' and 'innovation', when they really mean cheap gimmicks. The most treacherous moment was when *Zagat** named The Fat Duck in Bray as the best restaurant in the world!

But who cares about *Zagat*, when the only guide worth heeding is Michelin? Let us take a look and compare our countries' performance. At last count the score on restaurants boasting three Michelin stars was: France 26, England 3. Which tells us all we need to know.

Most of the top 'English' restaurants are actually foreign. Having no national cuisine of their own, they adopt everyone else's.** Chinese, Japanese, Indian, Italian and – of course – French restaurants reflect a society indebted to its immigrants. And thank goodness for those immigrants! Without them, they'd be locked into a diet of fried bread, treacle pudding and steak and kidney pud. You could put on ten kilos just thinking about it!

In Search of Modern British Cuisine

The 'chattering classes' won't accept that the only decent food is foreign, and puff on about the flowering of what they call Modern British Cuisine.

---

*Zagat Survey was founded by a New York couple in 1979 and rates restaurants on the basis of thousands of diners' experiences.
**The former Foreign Secretary Robin Cook once named Chicken Tikka Masala as the national dish.

I asked a colleague of my husband's where to find this and he sent to me to eat pig's trotters in the East End of London at a restaurant called St. John, where they urge customers to 'embrace your carcass', and say no to 'pink in plastic' meat. This devotion to offal is hardly innovative, for centuries our *charcuteries* have been preparing dishes from all parts of the pig, there is nothing modern about that, nor even British.

So I went back to my 'foodie' to ask for another suggestion. Something *un peu plus raffiné,* I said, not hearty peasant food. Something that encapsulates the essence of this *fameuse* Modern British Cuisine. Of course, he sent me to the Fat Duck. Best restaurant in the world, he crowed. Perverse and gimmicky, was my own assessment. Snail porridge (was this a sly dig at the French?), sardine sorbet, egg-and-bacon ice-cream served with a cup of green tea jelly. The best thing I ate there was a superb platter of French cheese and a bottle of Latricière Chambertin.

Try again, I said, please tell me where I should go for Modern British Cuisine. He looked perplexed. Then it came to him. Gastro pubs, he said, that is where you should go. What an ugly word, I said, gastro-pub, like gastro-porn, those colour food supplements that you drool over.

Etymologically, gastro-pub expresses the idea that you take the old benefits of the pub (drinking five pints of beer on an empty stomach, save a packet of pork scratchings) and marry them with the new gastronomy. *Bref,* eat as well as drink, what a groundbreaking idea! A typical dish might be saddle of rabbit with Swiss chard and polenta, a little bit Italian, a little bit vegetarian, a little bit French. They like their gastro-pubs so much you can now get special 'gastro-pub' ready meals in the supermarket, so you can eat them in your own TV lounge.

Let me talk you through the service I recently received in a gastro-pub. After a very ordinary piece of salmon, plonked on a plate with a nursery-food pile of vegetables, I ordered a chocolate pudding to cheer myself up. As she cleared my plate, the waitress engaged me in familiar banter. 'You didn't like that, then!' she joked. I was offended on many levels: the suggestion of intimacy between us; the idiotic British way of saying the opposite of what they mean, and the implication that I had been greedy in emptying my plate.

My conclusion? Modern British Cuisine does not exist. It is nothing but a marketing ploy, like the Ploughman's Lunch that I am told was invented in the seventies to describe a plate of bread with a lump of cheese.

Let us move on to something more appetizing:

French Restaurants

The best restaurants in England – more than three-quarters of the Michelin starred establishments – are still French. Take no notice of the *mauvaises langues* who say that our cuisine died thirty years ago, that our county is ossified in an unchanging round of *boeuf aux carottes* and *sole meunière*. The truth is evident. Once you've tired of the novelties, become sick of curry and raw fish and bored to death with pasta, there is only one thing you want to eat and that is classic French cuisine.

Just look at our glorious food heritage, rich in heroic acts of food martyrdom. Who can forget how the owner of the Relais de Porquerolles shot himself when he lost his Michelin star? Or how the gastronome Vatel impaled himself on his sword when the fish did not arrive at Chantilly during Louis XIV's visit? And can you imagine a British monarch spending his dying days threading dried morel mushrooms on a string the way Louis XIII did?

In contrast, the English had Queen Victoria working her way through a Christmas lunch, so heavy it always gave her indigestion. They have Winston Churchill, who would not tolerate discussion about food, preferring plain dishes washed down by plenty to drink (*plus ça change. . .*). Or modern-day MP Boris Johnson who says that 'food writing gets on his nerves'. Where we had Carème pronouncing that 'Pastry is the principal branch of architecture', here they had ploddy Mrs Beeton urging them to boil their mutton to death.

Apart from the food, the great joy of French restaurants in England is French waiters who are serious professionals and do not try to be your friend. They have been brought up to respect clients for being *exigeant,* and to despise them for being undiscriminating. So when the English describe a mediocre dish as 'lovely' or 'very nice' and never make a fuss about the *cuisson* of their steak, they are treated with the *hauteur* they deserve.

Eating at Strange Times

In France, lunch is at one, dinner is at eight, and that's the end of the matter.

Not in England, where you will often be offered a table at seven or nine o'clock so they can greedily cram in two seatings*; and lunch can be served at three in the afternoon.

In keeping with the twenty-four-hour grazing culture, you will see people ripping into sandwiches

---

*Not only that: in popular restaurants, you may need to confirm your reservation with a credit card. These people are so mercantile in all their dealings.

at all hours (on sale even at pharmacies!), bags of half-eaten fish and chips abandoned on night buses, monster size bars of Cadbury's milk chocolate sold alongside the morning papers and 'greasy spoon' cafés offering bacon and egg at all hours with the 'all day English breakfast'. No wonder their body clocks are so confused! And they eat dessert before cheese so that the cheese can 'take away the sweet taste', which shows how lowly is the role ascribed to English cheese!

The only strangely timed eating occasion that I approve of here is afternoon tea. *J'adore!* It reminds me of Angelina's on rue de Rivoli. Obviously, it is confusing to eat at four o'clock, but I prepare myself by taking only a light lunch before heading off to the Ritz or Fortnum's to enjoy the tiny egg sandwiches and scones with the piano playing in the background. It is really quite civilized and an ideal place for exchanging confidences with your girlfriends.

Here are my *astuces* to shop for food almost up to French standards:

* *Marks & Spencer* We still lament its passing on the boulevard Haussmann, and you feel a little *frisson* of nostalgia as you pick up their teatime fancies. The meat is less frightening than elsewhere.
* *Harrods Food Hall* I thought about taking a house just opposite so I could treat this as my corner shop but my husband feared for our

food bill. Hugely expensive version of Galeries Lafayettes where you can eat and buy anything.

* *Chocolate* All the best shops have French names: L'Artisan du Chocolat, Maison du Chocolat, Rococo.

* *Drive to Calais* There is of course one way of shopping for French food that I adore. Every few months, I go with two girlfriends in my *quatre quatre** and take the tunnel to the Calais hypermarkets, along with all the drunken Englishmen stocking up on alcohol at Eastenders. We lunch in a small bistro undiscovered by the 'booze cruisers' and return with *foie gras*, yoghurts, *confits*, coarse salt, coffee and Petit Lu biscuits. There is a shop in London where they sell Petit Lu biscuits, but it is obvious to me that they are not the same, so I prefer to bring back my own supply.

Maybe it's because I'm a Londoner . . .

I must admit that sometimes, when I am returning from summer after two months of *carottes rapées*, *salade niçoise*, perfect peaches, the delicious conformity of French seasonal food and the *grillades* of my local restaurant – a little revolutionary voice whispers in my ear . . . How about a takeaway curry? A cheese-and-pickle sandwich? Spring onion and

---

*Translator's note: affectionate term for four-wheel drive, which does not have the same diabolical connotations on the other side of the Channel.

chilli crisps? Even a bar of the chocolate-style confectionery Cadbury's Fruit and Nut? You see, you
cannot live in London without beginning to acquire
native tastes . . .

5

English Puritans

'An Englishman thinks he is moral when he is only
uncomfortable.'
George Bernard Shaw, Man and Superman

I adore life! Particularly since moving abroad, I awake each morning with a spring in my step, eager for every experience the day will hold! For is it not in our French nature to intensely celebrate our existence, and did we not invent the notion of *joie de vivre*? As I slip into a perfect spring jacket and head off to enjoy as good a lunch as I can hope to find (remember, I am not in France!), together with stimulating conversation and – *pourquoi pas?* – a little flirtation, I feel alive and *dynamique*!

What a shame that so many English people do not feel the same. I'm not saying they are all kill-joys, but they do like to deny themselves the *petits plaisirs* that make life worth living.

Having no talent for sex or food, they make a virtue of their deficiencies. What they really enjoy is going without. Rather than leave the office for a delicious lunch, they will pull out a Tupperware box of sandwiches. Instead of a *soirée sensuelle*, candlelit dinner followed by a night of love, they'll go to the country to strip wallpaper, walk in the rain and sleep in a freezing cold bed.

We all know these English puritans, we have all shuddered at their refusal to embrace the richness of daily life. Have you ever seen the austerity of a Methodist church? No incense, no rich robes, no mystery, so plain it makes you weep.

Here are some examples of English puritanism, many of them 'green' – which is penny-pinching envy dressed up as moral righteousness.

Eco Smugs

The English are delighted with their latest form of self-denial: carbon footprint counting. To compensate for all those fly-drive mini-breaks, they install low-wattage light bulbs, take tepid showers, and build wormeries to recycle their teabags, all performed in a bean-counting, mercenary way.

Now, before you correct me, I know that in France we were the first to do away with plastic carrier bags and legislate for eco-flush lavatories. But do we make a big fuss about it? *Non.* Do we behave like smug saviours of the planet? *Non*. Do we expect our political leaders to be filmed *cycling* to work (while an out-of-camera car follows up with the heavy attaché case)? *Bien sûr que non!*

And anyway, when you look at the emissions coming out of China, I always say that changing light bulbs is like fiddling while Rome burns.

Persecution of Big Cars

I make no apologies for driving what is described as a Chelsea tractor. Why would I not want to sit up high and protect my children? And yet I have been the victim of a bullying campaign, flyers stuffed on my windscreen by badly dressed 'eco-warriors' seeking to deny me my human right to drive whatever car I please. It's not as if I drive every day – I find it less fun than in Paris where driving is a sport and an opportunity for passionate exchanges – and I often take public transport. Pierre-Marie even takes the bus to work! That would never happen in Paris to someone in his position.

By the way, I'm thrilled by the extension of the congestion charge. Now I can drive slap bang into London whenever I feel like and *it's completely free*! *Merci*, Ken!

Cyclists

We cycle in France. We do it properly, as a weekend sport, wearing bright Lycra clothing on multi-geared mountain bikes. The English cycle because they are cheap and because they like to arrive at dinner and make a great show of pulling off their helmets and luminous green bands to show what great citizens they are. The women look appalling, of course, hair flattened, scruffy clothes, jangling padlock keys and bike lights in their sensible backpacks. And everyone is supposed to admire them for being too mean to dress properly and pay for a taxi.

Self-righteous Food

In France we like food that tastes good. English puritans don't care what it tastes like as long as it has a label showing it's from the right place. This is called 'sourcing'. The ideal label is 'organic' (much overrated as we know), and from a farmer whose name and address they can drop to their guests. They love shops like Planet Organic which make a great fuss about overpriced cheese and produce that is only what you'd find in the most basic French market. They like to claim allergies, and buy bags of dried pulses which they stuff in the back of the cupboard and never cook.

'This Needs Eating Up'

The English are at their happiest when making do, and love eating leftovers. Where we would throw last night's supper in the *poubelle*, the English will have it for lunch, which makes them feel virtuous for saving money. It is also an excuse for gluttony. 'Shame to let it go to waste,' they say, as if they are doing everyone a favour by hoovering up the cold remains of a treacle pudding.

'Put On a Sweater'

Although they enjoy complaining about their wretched climate, the English like being cold. Rather than turn up the heating, they will urge everyone to 'put on a sweater'. It reminds them of their own chilly childhoods, where at draughty boarding schools they wore short trousers throughout the winter. In a heatwave, they can't wait for normal conditions to be restored, for the skies to grow grey, so they can pile on the anoraks and cheerfully commiserate with each other.

I always take a pashmina when invited to an English home, even in summer. Chances are you'll be sitting in the cold dungeon dining room. I also have an electric blanket which I pack if we are invited to the country.

Queuing

The favourite English pastime: it's free, it makes people feel self-righteous, and adds value to whatever they are waiting for. Before the Harrods sale, they stand for hours in line on the cold *trottoir*, and even spend the night there in a sleeping bag! It could not happen in France. We would just arrive at opening time and push our way to the front.

My neighbour Bee was very upset in Paris when a woman pushed in ahead of her at the queue for an exhibition at the Beaubourg. 'But she was so well dressed,' she said, as if it was a 'chav' thing to try to get ahead. I explained to her that French people are too intelligent to hang around at the back of a queue. It's the same on the roads. Of course you use the hard shoulder to overtake in a traffic jam if your lane isn't moving, *c'est tout à fait normal*. Yet here there would be angry accusations of 'sneaking up on the inside' and such nonsense.

Caravanning

Even quite well-off English families go on caravan holidays, which is a shock to us.* They love having to

---

Madame l'ex-ministre for foreign affairs Margaret Beckett has a caravan! Hard to imagine a French minister being so *ringard!*

'make do' with miniature clothes drawers, and draw satisfaction from driving their own cans of baked beans across France, whiling away the journey with pleasant thoughts of how much they are saving on food. Purist caravanners reject multi-facility sites in favour of small bourgeois 'certified locations' more in keeping with the austere ethos of self-denial. I have heard English people say how enjoyable it is to do the *vaisselle* at the communal wash block. *Vraiment, ces Calvinistes!*

Politicians Must Also 'Go Without'

In France, we accept that the government is housed in sumptuous palaces, that the fresh flower bill for the Élysée runs into hundreds of thousands, that *M. le Président* has use of a Provençal château for his holidays and a state apartment for his mistress. It is like the Pope in the golden splendour of the Vatican, the *maison de fonction* comes with the job.

The English will not have it. Not content with 'going without' themselves, they want to make sure their politicians do the same. The cost of the wall-paper used in the Chancellor's office; the Prime Minister's tropical holidays in pop stars' mansions, the hairdressing bill for his accompanying spouse: all are exposed by the English press and chewed over by the disapproving public, who would rather see them 'making do' with a rainy cottage in Scotland and Homebase wallpaper, preferably obtained half-price after queueing in the Christmas sales.

My tips / *mes astuces:*

* Show them how to love life, possibly by dressing better.
* Suggest they move to France, where all food is properly 'sourced' and they won't have to read the labels.*
* Ingratiate yourself with a puritan by taking him a gift wrapped in newspaper.
* Keep quiet about your 4x4, your long-haul holidays, and your patio heater.

6

The English at Work

'The maxim of the British people is
"Business as Usual".'
Winston Churchill

In France we have a civilized approach to work. It is part of life, not the point of it. Not so in money-loving England, where it is an obsession. What do you do? Business going well? Did you get a good bonus? These are all acceptable openings when conversing with strangers. Such terrible manners!

It is generally true that while English people move to France for pleasure, French people move to England to work. Why else would you bother?

There is nothing I like better than sharing an intimate midweek *dîner en couple* with Pierre-Marie. We sit down, perhaps over a *tarte* from Paul, and exchange our news. I tell him about the children, the latest exhibition at the Tate Modern, the failure of the *Mairie* to collect our recycling bags that morning. And he tells me tales about the English at work. I'd like to share his observations with you now. I have the good fortune *not* to be tied to the office, but Pierre-Marie has given me such a good insight, I feel I'm almost there beside him.

English Duplicity

The prevailing mood of English office life is one of breezy *bonhomie*. In contrast to our *très correct* reserve, they are instantly friendly and accommodating, smiling all the time and urging you to 'call me Tony'.

Then they turn round and fire you without a moment's notice.

Behaviour in Meetings

What the English will always say in meetings is 'yes'. Yes, they love the work, yes they think that's a great idea, yes, why not? Yes absolutely.

Do not be fooled.

They will then follow up with the killer twist. Yes, they love the work, only don't you think it would be better to do it this way (i.e. start again). Yes, the sales have vastly improved (except they're down on last year). Yes, absolutely (by which they mean, *absolument pas*!).

This dishonesty is very wearing and makes it almost impossible to do business with them. Why can't they be like us and just say '*Non*' to everything?

An irritating new variation on 'Yes' is 'Yeah, yeah, yeah' repeated in quick succession. This will be used to cut you short when you are explaining something or when they think you are being boring (the greatest crime in English business).

You will say, 'If I could refer you to page 437 of the analysis, in the nineteenth clause, where you will find it explained how the exponential . . .'

Then your English interlocutor will say, 'Yeah, yeah, yeah,' and hold his hand up in an attempt to stop you continuing.

Although the English can't bear us being boring, they can be very boring and repetitive themselves. For instance when they are introduced to you. We say 'Bonjour', or 'Hello'. Just the once. They will say, 'Hi, hello, hi, pleased to meet you, yes, hi, hi, yes, yes, hi.' Over-effusive, and treacherous. It is really most *énervant*.

Lack of Rigour

English business meetings are anarchic and confusing. Ignoring the agenda, people veer off at a tangent and make 'funny' remarks throughout. The most respect is accorded to the person who tells the best joke, and decisions are rushed and badly thought through.

In France, we have a far better system. Respect for *les droits de l'homme* insists that every person may express his opinion, at great length, with passion and elegance. And then the most senior person says what must be done. Honour is satisfied, democracy upheld, and the boss makes the decisions, which is how it should be.

Bonding Exercises

Picture a conference held by a multinational French company. A fine hotel in Deauville, excellent wines, and every division hosted at its own table. Why would you want to sit next to someone from Germany or Japan? You're in the same room as them, that is quite enough mixing.

For the English, this just will not do. The urge to become intimately connected with one's colleagues is carried to ridiculous lengths, and not just by drinking Anglo-Saxon quantities at the hotel bar. Marie-Cha's husband told me an extraordinary story of a weekend he had spent in an icy Welsh river. At vast expense, he and his fellow senior managers had been sent off to build a raft together under the messianic gaze of a 'leadership consultant'.

'I am a statistician,' he said. 'Why do I need to know how to knock pieces of wood together?'

The English have fallen big time for this global confidence trick that falls under the domaine of 'management consultancy'. I fear this takes its origins from the protestant lay preachers: simplistic homilies spelt out for the common man, whereas we remain Catholic, mysterious and autocratic – the Pope or the boss dictates, and we fall in. So I suppose we only have ourselves to blame: we expelled the Huguenots, and now they return to haunt us!

Other bonding exercises include imaginary role-play situations, getting 'bladdered' at the office party and wearing a clown's nose on 'Red Nose Day'. All deeply uncomfortable for a French person who has his personal dignity and does not take kindly to being made a fool of.

Management Jargon and Globish

How right we were to set up the Académie Française: a superb guard dog of an institution, defending the French language against foreign imports. Most pernicious of all is the imprecise language of Anglo-Saxon business culture.

It took a Frenchman to cut through the nonsensical way that the English speak in business meetings, with all its silly codes and nuances, and failure to be direct. Jean-Claude Nerrières has come up with the concept of 'Globish'*. I am glad to say it forbids the use of jokes!

The Overseas Call Centre

I have heard people complain about customer service in France, but at least you can understand what they are saying (although sometimes one does have a little difficulty with the Marseille twang or – heaven forfend! – a Quebecois! I am digressing now, but was so grateful for the subtitles for the film *The Barbarian Invasions*).

English companies used to base their call centres in Newcastle, on the pretext that this accent was the most friendly, though really it allowed them pay lower wages. Now they have taken their penny-pinching even further by putting customers' calls through to India! Imagine my frustration at trying to explain my hard disk failure to Sharon in Delhi, and being unable to understand a word she says! Can you imagine Wanadoo customers having to ring the Cameroons?

*'Globish' is a reduced English Lexicon of 1500 words, promoted for international communication.

Entrepreneurs

Not only did we give the English their national anthem*, we also gave them the word that sums up their business style†, and my goodness how they pride themselves on their entrepreneurial spirit! They pronounce it with a flourish: 'He's an entrepreneur!' and the nod of respect always accorded to anyone who makes money. For us of course, an entrepreneur is just what the word means: a tradesperson who 'takes between', and nothing to get excited about. The humblest plumber is an *entrepreneur* with his own *entreprise*.

The Office Lunch

In France, we know there is no point in trying to reach anybody between the hours of twelve and two. The right of every person to sit down to a proper three-course lunch is a triumph of French civilization. Who has not nodded '*Bon appétit*' to a group of builders,

---

*'God Save the Queen' is adapted from 'Grand dieu sauve le Roi', written by the duchesse de Brinon and set to music by Lully in 1686, to celebrate Louis XIV's recovery from haemorrhoids.
†President Bush is reported to have once said 'the French have no word for entrepreneur', but this is probably just another piece of English anti-American propaganda.

engaged in animated conversation around an improvised trestle table erected *en plein chantier*?

Alas, things are very different in the land of the
sandwich. Hunched over their computers, office
workers drop bits of panini and oily fragments of
crisps on to their keyboards throughout the day,
washed down by insipid cups of tea prepared in big
mugs bearing jokey messages. Sometimes they may go
out to the pub, where they have to balance plates of
microwaved food in one hand and a pint glass in the
other, which is not conducive to good digestion.

Business lunches between young people are monas-
tic affairs washed down by water. Those over forty, on
the other hand, drink heavily, eyes popping out of
their big red faces as they lament the decline of the
'serious lunches' they used to enjoy in the eighties.
In neither case is a civilized single glass of wine
an option.

Commuting

The English like to live as far as possible from their
place of work, particularly once they have children.
This gives the wife an excuse to give up work – 'My
salary wouldn't even cover the train fares' – and the
husband the chance to play the martyr by leaving
home, whey-faced, at 5 a.m. and returning to find

his wife in bed, where she has been all day on account of her depression (and who wouldn't be depressed, so far from the city?).

At risk of praising the French model *again*, here is where we really do know better. We will settle for a modest apartment near our place of work, that suits our lifestyle. We are far too intelligent to opt for a two-hour commute for the sake of a few more square metres and a patch of garden. The only person I know in France who commutes (from Troyes to Paris) is an Englishman. He cannot believe the quality of the trains, and says if it were in England they would be crying in gratitude.

7

Transport

'Rush hour: that hour when traffic is almost
at a standstill'

J. B. Morton

Public Transport

It is a miracle that anyone in England ever gets
to work at all. Like all Londoners, I have stood
on underground platforms, suffering the usual
delays before cramming myself into a carriage packed
with big English people eating food out of paper
bags and wearing discordant clothing (so unlike
the neat monochrome figures one encounters in the
Paris metro).

'In France, this would not be tolerated!' I said to
Marie-Cha, as we turned our faces to avoid breathing in the fumes of a bacon-and-egg roll, to which
she replied 'And in France, we do not eat hot breakfast while standing pressed against the body of a
stranger.'

Worst of all is the way nobody complains.
Phlegmatic as cattle, the English let go of the sticky

plastic poles to glance at their watches, then stick themselves back, showing no emotion.

At least a tube journey is relatively short (unless you happen to break down in a tunnel for three hours, in which case you may eventually be led out along the tracks like rats after the Pied Piper). I am told that commuter trains from outside London are just as crowded, with standing room only, even in the toilet compartment, although you pay heavily for the privilege.

If you want a lesson on the perils of privatization, try booking a rail ticket in England. In France, we go on the SNCF website, everything centralized, rational and reasonably priced. In England, every railway line is owned by a different company, you will get lost in a sea of websites and eventually succeed in buying a ticket from London to Leeds (a mere 280 kilometres) for £175. This is not a joke.

The English like the inefficiency of their transport because it gives them rich scope for jokes and head-shaking at the pub. One inch of snow, and the whole system falls apart ('Cheers mate!'). The wrong sort of leaves on the lines again, ('Dear me, mine's a pint, thanks love'). You'll never believe how long it took me to get in this morning, three and a half hours, and that was before the strike, ('oh well, what are you drinking?').

Obedient Drivers

Freewheeling in many ways, the English are deeply conformist when it comes to driving. Respect for the rules has been described as the essence of Englishness, and *mon dieu*, how they respect the rules of the road! Obediently sticking to the speed limits, avoiding the bus lanes, fastidiously respecting those yellow boxes: . . . They wouldn't survive for five minutes in Paris, although when you look at the crippling punishment they risk, you begin to understand why: stiff fines for forgetting to pay the congestion charge, deceitfully hidden speed cameras ready to slap points on one's licence, zealous parking wardens. Add to this the constant gridlock on the M25 and the highest fuel costs in Europe, and you can see how the English motorist has become an emasculated shadow of his former self.

When drivers stop to let pedestrians cross, it is not because they are courteous but because they have been beaten into submission, and lack the *chacun pour soi* spirit that is necessary to survive on French roads.

One thing I miss from home is being able to tell where a car's owner comes from. It is satisfying to

*Translator's note: Hortense is referring to the last two digits on a French car's registration plate. A 75, '*soixante- quinze*', is

know from his 75 number plate* that it is a Parisian who has cut you up, or that of course he is driving *comme un con** because he's a 93 (pronounced *neuf-trois*) from the unfashionable suburbs of Seine-Saint-Denis or a 14 from Calvados. Spend a weekend in a French country town and a glance at the licence plates in the high street will instantly reveal whether it is popular with Parisians or just another gloomy outpost of *la France profonde*. It enforces our pronounced sense of territory.

In England, you are deprived of this pleasure. Instead, the number plate tells you how old the car is. So, you will hear someone saying, disapprovingly, 'He drives an F reg Ford'**, or, enviously, 'He turned up in his brand new Jag.' I mention this because it took me a long time to understand the significance.

Although they pride themselves on being careful drivers, the English are not good *motoring citizens*. Unlike us, they do not flash their lights at oncoming vehicles to warn them of a police checkpoint. Nor do they give vent to their feelings in a healthy exchange

always noted with approval by Parisians, and with loathing by everyone else.

*Translator's note: like an idiot. *Con* is the generic slang term for anyone or anything the French consider beneath them, and therefore widely used.

**Letters were used until 2001 when it changed to numbers.

of gestures and strong words, the way we do. Instead, they stew in silent fury, internalizing their anger until it boils over, at which point they get out of the car and beat another driver to a pulp. This is known as 'road rage'.

Taxis

There are two sorts in London: minicabs, which are always driven by ethnic minorites, and black cabs that are only driven by white men.

Minicab drivers are like our own taxi drivers, and not too talkative. You have to give them directions, or consult an A–Z map with them to try and find out where you are going.

Black-cab drivers are notoriously opinionated and will take advantage of the journey to tell you what is wrong with the country. This is to distract you from the frightening sight of the meter clocking up the cost.

Londoners love black cabs, and claim it is what they miss most when they leave town. They are flattered by the intimacy of its confessional: within the cab, it is 'You and me against the world', for the cabbie is a self-employed businessman with the entrepreneurial spirit the English so admire. Their off-the-cuff remarks are often quoted by upper-class professionals to prove they are in touch with the common man.

You must never tell a black-cab driver which route to take, otherwise he might throw you out. A common sight is a black cab U-turning in the middle of a traffic jam, and speeding off in a new direction, for the unique turning circle of his vehicle and his knowledge of shortcuts are unparalleled.

The black-cab driver has a new enemy in the West End: the rickshaw cyclist. These slightly built boys with overdeveloped thighs can pull their weighty cargo of shrieking drunks down short-cut passages too narrow for cars.

Black cabs not only drive on the wrong side of the road, they also have the wrong signals. The yellow light is illogically switched *on* when it is available, contrary to the proper way of doing things.

Cyclists

I have dealt with cyclists in my chapter about puritans, since the bicycle here is not so much a means of transport as a self-righteous lifestyle statement.

8

Money, Money, Money!

'Englishmen: all rich.'

Gustave Flaubert, Dictionary of Commonplaces

***

'Any Frenchman who wants to make money goes to
Britain or America these days. In France, it is virtually
impossible to build up a fortune any more.'

Claude Taittinger, in an interview in the Sunday Times

May I echo the sentiments of Jacques Chirac, who said there was nothing to envy or copy in the British model? Whilst I don't wish to bite the hand that feeds me (Pierre-Marie says that the English tax regime is *très intéressant* for foreigners, and who am I to argue?), the huge gulf between rich and poor in this country is an affront to our republicanism.

As proof of how unmaterialistic the French are, just consider how the late anti-poverty campaigner Abbé Pierre was elected 'most popular man in France' for nine consecutive years, until modesty impelled him to withdraw from the poll. We are suspicious of people who make money, and naturally approve of tax inspectors checking out lists to see who has bought expensive houses, cars, boats, etc. (If certain of us who are *plus aisés* have adjusted our investments accordingly, with judicious use of offshore accounts and careful storage of art treasures behind the blank façades of our 'give nothing away apartments', this has nothing to do with laundering, merely a way of preserving our *patrimoine*.)

Believe me, there is no such reticence in England! If ever I felt a *little* uncomfortable at just how well Pierre-Marie was doing in Paris, here in London we feel almost poor! How can you not, when the papers scream about record city bonuses and tell you exactly how much your colleague made out of the latest takeover. Every day there is a story on house prices, to make those of us who rent our homes feel like beggars at the feast. You can go online to find out how much your neighbours paid for their apartment, how much a company director got paid last year. The streets are thickly parked with luxury cars. It's enough to send you rushing back to France, and to hell with that 50 percent tax rate, just for the sake of a little discretion.

There are terrible costs to all this money slushing around. Here are some examples:

Greedy Discontent

In France, we know that happiness is found in daily pleasures. Buying mushrooms from the market, the moment of the *apéritif*, the contemplation of a well dressed woman. Accessible pleasures, open to all.

In England, this has been lost beneath a miasma of nagging discontent. I should be getting more. I wish I was her. I must have that. Get me to the shops. Book me a mini-break. This envious greed is fed by newspapers divided into sections to feed different aspirations: the 'Money' section, obviously, but also 'Homes' (why can't I afford that one?), 'Travel (I can't believe I still haven't been on a safari to Botswana), 'Culture'(I really need a better TV to see that film).

The work-and-money cult has created a new 'must-have' which the English call 'me-time'. This narcissistic term refers to activities I engage in without a second thought: the spa, a lie down with a book, a solitary stroll in the park. For the French, all time is 'me-time', we don't need to give it a silly name.

Debt Addiction

Would I like to borrow £10,000? No thank you, I would not. And I tear up another letter that comes addressed to me, with a cheque in my name, offering 'cheap' money. It is an outrage. If I could be bothered I would write to them and remind them that having an overdraft in France is a criminal offence. I was brought up never to borrow money from a bank, and I do not intend to start now.

Sycophantic Banks

It's impossible to open a bank account when you arrive in England. It works like this: you need a utility bill as proof of your address, which you don't yet have because you've just arrived, which is why you need to open a bank account. It is a chicken-and-egg situation, the philosophical possibilities of which were unfortunately lost on the bovine bank clerk to whom I was trying to explain my frustration.

Once they've got you, however, they won't let you go. You will be bombarded with letters from agencies informing you of changes to 'relationship support centres', making them sound like marriage guidance counsellors, which is accurate as the English love their money more than their spouses.

Pray you never need to speak to anyone at the PO Box Number that pretends to manage your account: you will be kept waiting on a premium rate line until someone introduces herself using her first name (do I care what she's called?) and be over-familiar. Once when I had to organize a quarterly rent payment by telephone, Tina in the north of England made me repeat the amount three times. 'How much? For three months! I could buy a flat for that!'

Loyalty cards

My *porte-monnaie* has lost its elegant lines, bulging with storecards that 'reward' me whenever I spend money in a high-street chain. It's all part of the 'village' conspiracy, to make you feel you 'belong' to a commercial organization. Your loyalty is measured out into points, exchangeable for little treats. Because you're worth it. How do they know what I am worth? My loyalty is to people I know, not to cynical marketing departments.

The 'Free' Market

The English remain convinced that a free market is a good thing, but it leads to confusion and too many choices. Why would I want a hundred cheap and nasty imported handbags when I can get one exquisitely crafted by Chanel? Why should I have to choose between eight electricity suppliers? As long as I can switch it on I don't care where it comes from. Why drink wine shipped from the other side of the world when we have our own wonderful vineyards?

Ségolène Royal showed the correct attitude when she arranged for schoolchildren in her constituency to be given a pair of slippers each made by the local factory. A dynamic initiative to boost local business and make the children feel treasured, and none of the money disappearing into foreign pockets.

Marrying for Money

There is no *séparation de biens* in English marriages, only an optional prenuptial agreement that counts for nothing in the British courts. When the law changed a few years ago, cast-off wives found they could lay claim to half their husband's fortune, and London soon became the divorce capital of the world. The quickest way for a woman to make money now is to marry someone wealthy and then divorce them. The papers are full of stories of such gold-diggers, showing photos of grim-faced families whose expectations have been crushed by a senile fool marrying his carer.

Thank goodness that in France, a child's rights to inherit from her parents remains sacrosanct. Should Papa decide to remarry, at least my share of the *manoir* would remain unviolated. Not to mention my allocation of those *Luxembourgeois* accounts that he thinks I don't know about. It gives true meaning to the term *patrimoine*, Father's money, destined for his descendants, and therefore – happily! – coming my way. And French law will not permit a dying person to leave money to his doctor. So take my advice, if you have expectations, on no account allow your parents to follow you to *la perfide Albion*.*

Never Marry for Money: a Personal Note

I could never have married for money, it is so vulgar. Marriage is a spiritual bond of body and soul, a life-long voyage of two kindred souls. Though naturally, one has to use one's head as well as one's heart when settling on a marriage partner. Pierre-Marie didn't have a *sou* to his name when we met, but he had graduated 34th in his *promotion* at ENA and I was instantly attracted by the power of his mind. The first time we met was at a mutual friend's apartment where I was staying while following a *stage*† at the

*Translator's note: scholarly footnotes abound in other books about the origins of this expression. Suffice it to know that *la perfide Albion* is shorthand for the many forms of treachery practised by the English.

†Translator's note: a *stage* is an unpaid work experience placement, an essential step towards a successful career. The quality of one's child's *stage* depends entirely on whom one knows. This unashamed networking is called *le piston*.

Banque du Louvre. He had been asked by his friend to check the internal repairs that were required, and as he made the inspection, he made no notes. The following day he sent in a full inventory, in tiny, neat handwriting, everything committed to memory. A first class brain. I knew then that he would be *l'homme de ma vie**.

*Translator's note: one of the things we love about the French is their unsmiling sincerity. Unlike us, they can refer to the 'man/woman of my life' without making a joke of it.

9

The English at Play

'To be able to fill leisure intelligently is the last product
of civilization, and at present very few people have
reached this level.'

Bertrand Russell, The Conquest of Happiness, 1930

The English are great believers in 'fun', which does not translate into French.

We have specific pleasures and amusements (a well turned *chausson de pommes*, for example, or a round of *boules*) but not one generic fit-all term. So the English will say, 'she's good fun', 'it's a really fun restaurant'. An office party and a Shakespeare production are both 'enormous fun', and competitive sport is just another rollercoaster of laughs, if we are to believe what one mother said to me as we were watching our daughters in a dance competition: 'There is only one rule in these competitions, and that's to have fun.' For my daughter the first rule is to win.

Let us examine some ways in which the English have fun:

1. *Drinking*

'They remove boredom with alcohol.' *Abbé le Blanc*

'They don't like to see us with drink taken, out of control.' *Advice to British servicemen in France, 1944*

The most reliable way for the English to have fun is to drink to excess. This is something we find hard to accept, because for us, drunkenness is *la honte*, deep shame. In England, the shame is in *not* joining in, in refusing to make yourself ill by drinking a bottle of wine on an empty stomach.

I tried to explain once that for us, wine is *un plat*, part of the dining ritual, that it cannot exist in isolation. I was met with utter incomprehension. For the English, wine, beer, spirits are all the same, all there to be randomly consumed in the pursuit of 'fun' until you slur your words, knock over your glass or stumble into the gutter.

Walk down a London street on a Friday night, and you could be in a Hogarth etching of Gin Alley. Scantily dressed young women and men with shirts untucked from their trousers lurch across the street bellowing with laughter, falling off their high heels, faces shiny from ten vodka cocktails or sinking the gallon.*

No pub is without its regulars who give each other a hard time if they miss a session. 'Where's your (sick) note?' Older people are more likely to do their drinking at home, tut-tutting at TV documentaries about young binge drinkers as they steadily knock back the Jacob's Creek.

At my Saturday morning gym class, my teacher always begins by asking, 'Any injuries? Any pregnancies? Any hangovers?' Getting drunk is just part of the weekly routine.

Here are some memorable images of drunken England:

• Front-page newspaper photo of a middle-aged manager asleep on railway tracks, following an office party.

• Traces of vomit, especially next to walls near to undergound stations.

• The sounds of chinking glass as the English put out their recyling bags bulging with shameful evidence.

• The English football hooligan, that international icon, bare-bellied, belligerent, holding four cans of

*Four litres of beer, standard measure for the average Englishman.

lager and singing a lewd song insulting the sexuality of the opponent team.

• PBAB. Can you believe that English invitations will often include these initials, after RSVP? It means please bring a bottle, instructing you to furnish supplies for your own binge drinking!

• Hog-whimpering, rat-arsed, shit-faced, bladdered, squiffy. . . the English vocabulary of drunkenness is unrivalled in its richness. Whereas all we have is *saoul* and *bourré*, and that gesture that involves putting a clenched fist to our face and pretending to twist our nose around.

2. *Sport: the Importance of Heroic Failure*

The English pride themselves on being 'good losers' and insist they practise sport for 'fun' and not to win. This offends my French soul. We play sport with passion, the way we approach all aspects of life, and do not mess around pretending it doesn't matter if we lose.

As usual with the English, though, it's not quite as it seems. They pretend they don't mind losing, but in reality they are viciously competitive. As can be seen in savage games of croquet fought in the genteelest surroundings.

Here are some examples of the shambling amateurism of English sport, the silly pretence that winning is not the point and that it is 'taking part that matters'. It defies all Cartesian logic.

WEARING THE WRONG CLOTHES

When my neighbour Bee saw Pierre-Marie setting out for a jog in his Lycra shorts, new white trainers, polo shirt from *Le Racing* club in Paris and coordinated headband she laughed her head off. I asked her what was so funny. 'All the gear and no idea,' she said. This is the standard British insult for anyone who has taken the trouble to acquire the correct clothes for their sporting activity. Her husband Hereward also goes running, and wears baggy joggers, a ripped T-shirt and a pair of battered old plimsolls. It was the same story when we were invited away for a country weekend. Naturally, we were kitted out in full tennis kit. Our opponents on court were wearing open sandals and kaftans and could barely lift a racket, but hooted with laughter and declared the match 'tremendous fun'. To my mind there is nothing amusing about not doing things properly.

'HENMAN HILL'

'The English instinctively admire any man who has no talent and is modest about it' *James Agate*

Although they invented tennis, the English haven't had a decent player for years. Instead of being ashamed, they take perverse pleasure in this failure, and every year when the hapless Tim Henman attempts the Wimbledon tournament, his devoted fans assemble outside the club to cheer him on, wearing embarrassing hats, waving banners, knowing full well he will never get beyond the quarter final. His inevitable elimination sets the tone of Wimbledon commentary, which is peppered with hang-dog humour 'Poor old England, still at least we're good sports and it's taking part that matters.'

SCHOOL SPORTS DAYS

English infantilism is apparent in the school sports day that marks the end of the summer term. They have a 'sack race' where the children must run standing in a sack, and an 'egg-and-spoon race' where they have to balance a golf ball on a teaspoon. There is also a race for the parents. If this took place in France, the parents would of course come to the event suitably dressed in sports gear, but in England, you must remain in your *tenue de ville*, kicking off your shoes to run barefoot. It is most undignified. To cater for the English fondness for failure there has been a movement to ban winning from sports days. That way, everyone can be a failure.

MISSING THE TARGET

The English like to put themselves in a position where winning is not an option. To 'shoot a sitting duck' is considered bad form, because it is too easy. Far better to fail by aiming at birds flying way beyond the range of your gun fire. Likewise with fishing, an Englishman will sit there all day not catching anything, then pack up and go home as soon as dusk arrives, when the fish are practically throwing themselves out of the water. English people always laugh at our trout fishing in France, saying the pond is too small and full of fish and therefore too easy. But only a fool would want to spend all day motionless on a stool just for the sake of saying 'It was really tough'.

SCOTT OF THE ANTARCTIC

The ultimate sporting failure, he is top of the list of English heroes because of the way he failed to reach the South Pole. Had he been French, we would have quietly forgotten about him. You don't achieve greatness by celebrating your failures.

CRICKET

Obscure, incomprehensible and looking back to a better age, cricket appeals on every level to the English sports lover. It is an exercise in self-flagellation as

England 'loses the Ashes' once again to a former colony it once patronized. The class divide is irresistible, a reminder of how lanky lords of the manor used to play against short plebians on the village green, and may the best team win (though of course, both sides would rather lose, and obviously it's taking part that matters).

Freddy Flintoff is a popular captain, as (a) he would have been from the plebian village side (in refreshing contrast to most of the players and commentators who are upper class ex-'public' school*), and (b) his real name is Andrew. Freddy is a nickname, and the English are inordinately fond of nicknames.

Cricket is a popular subject for the 'heroic failure' genre of books, where writers compete to appear the most useless at sport.

It wasn't always this way. The Duke of Wellington remarked as he was watched a game of cricket that 'Waterloo was won on the playing fields of Eton'. It makes it doubly painful for them now, to see how things have been downhill ever since.

FOOTBALL

The English have made an art out of loser-worship and some football fans deliberately choose to support a weak team. 'It's no fun supporting Chelsea,' they'll say, 'because they always win.'

Apparently it's more 'fun' to pick an obscure team at the bottom of the third division, because then you can rail against their appalling game, and chastise them, and at the same time, yourself for being fool enough to support them. *Ah, ces Anglais* – crazy masochists!

FOOTNOTE TO SPORT (ENGLISH *vs* FRENCH SPORT)

It has been pointed out to me that the word 'sport' did not enter the French vocabulary until quite recently, and that we 'stole' all our sports from the English. I admit that we imported *les petits jeux anglais*, in the same way that the English stole the idea of military gymnastics from the Germans.

Whatever the history, we have now overtaken our poor neighbours in every field. We have had the sense to put proper funding into municipal sport, thereby providing English teams with their best football players. And it's just as well they're such good losers – they certainly need that famous sense of humour when it's time to hand out the Olympic medals!

ÉCOLE DE CIRQUE

There is one uniquely French sporting tradition that I would like to pass on to our English friends, in the spirit of 'giving back' if you like, in return for the football, tennis, cycling, etc. at which we now so roundly defeat them. This is the *école de cirque*, the delightful blend of athleticism and elegance manifested by our acrobats. Our sports club in Paris (*Le Racing*, famous for its noble origins) was the first to found such a school, and circus classes have become a favourite activity for every child on Club Med holidays. For some reason, my English friends always find the idea ridiculous, which suprises me as they love dressing up in shiny outfits for their silly pantomimes.

3. *Silly Games*

'To behold the Englishman at his best one should watch him play tip-and-run'* *Ronald Firbank, The Flower Beneath the Foot*

The English find it hard to connect with each other. Serious conversation is discouraged, so they fall back on trite chit-chat, recounting their daily lives in interminable detail. 'You'll never guess what happened to me today?' they'll say, then go on to explain how they failed to switch the kettle on, or missed their tube connection.

*Chaotic, improvised form of cricket, formerly popular on picnic outings.

To reduce their exposure to this level of conversation, the English have invented silly games. These take many forms, though all are utterly pointless.

Favourite English silly games:

Board games.

The pub quiz. We have *café philo*, to passionately debate the meaning of life. They argue about who scored the winning goal in the 2004 European cup semi-final.

Jigsaws.

Charades.

Blind man's Buff (a rare chance to touch each other).

Fancy Dress Parties. If we were going to a *bal masqué*, we would do it properly and go to a specialist theatrical dress hire shop. The English take pride in throwing together a shambolic outfit, because it's 'more fun'. So while we would hire full naval uniform to go as a sea captain, they would just tie on a spotty hanky and kid's eye-patch to go as a pirate.

10

At Home with the English

'An Englishman's home is his castle.'

Anon.

* * *

'The spread of personal ownership is in harmony with
the deepest instincts of the British people.'

Nigel Lawson, Chancellor of the Exchequer, 1988

The English are absurdly proud of their homes.
They spend more than anyone else in Europe on
them, and are always 'doing them up' – shopping
for furniture, hanging round at DIY stores, poring
over colour schemes in design magazines. When
they send invitations to parties, the cards carry the
words 'At Home' engraved in a flamboyant script, as
if no destination could be more *fabuleux* for their
lucky guests.

And yet you might be forgiven for asking the
question, why? What is all the fuss about?

When I lived in France, I used to say that *Paris,
c'est ma maison.* I treated the city as if it were my

apartment. Londoners do not have this relationship with their city; they scuttle back to their homes, to pull the curtains, tuck themselves away and get cosy. All the time and attention they don't spend on their personal appearance is directed into beautifying their four walls, a fascinating piece of transference that I could write an entire book about.

You will forgive me if I confine my observations to the London home, since this is where you will be living as a French immigrant. An estimated 300,000 French people live in the UK, and as far as I can work out, none of them live outside the capital (unlike the English in France, who all gravitate to *la province*).

My First Impression of London

Unlike Paris, so neatly confined within its boundary *périphérique*, London is an ungainly, sprawling place. For us, *une bonne adresse* is an imposing building on a grand boulevard, but the best London houses are built around quiet squares, hidden away from view. Moving out of the smartest *quartiers*, you will encounter streets of identical joined-up prole-tarian houses stretching out in all directions. No grandeur, and every house with uniform railings and funny windows that slide up and down and cannot be thrown open. There is no privacy, front and back gardens are overlooked from all sides.

The other shock to the newcomer is the social mix. Even the smartest areas contain looming council estates. The English pretend to like what they call living 'cheek by jowl' as if it could possibly be a good thing for millionaires to live next door to poor people.* With temptation on everyone's doorstep it's no wonder that house burglary† is a national sport. In Paris, we avoid the problem by not allowing council housing in the city: troublemakers have to take the bus in from the suburbs.

The Property Ladder

The English are obsessed by home ownership, and cannot walk past an estate agent's window without checking to see what they might afford and salivating at what they cannot.

In France, we buy a house because we have enough money, and we are going to live in it for at least ten

---

*To disguise this unsavoury fact, Londoners retreat into nostalgic olde worlde mode, pretending that their dangerous city is a harmless collection of 'villages'. So Brackenbury village, Highgate village, Clapham village . . . not villages at all.
†'Routine burglary' is so common the police may not get to visit for several days, if at all.

years. The English buy a house even if they have no money – they borrow it all from the bank in order to climb 'the property ladder'. An extraordinary idea. And where does this ladder lead, I asked my neighbour once. Does it lead to heaven, like Jacob's ladder? In fact, it simply leads to more expensive homes, debts multiplying at every turn.

In France, we are wary of the *marchands de bien*, dealers who buy and sell houses for profit, but in England everyone is a *marchand de bien*. The property ladder is the very essence of Englishness: a fusion of greedy profiteering and stay-at-home cosiness.

A House or a 'Flat'?

If you want to entertain at home, you must take an apartment, which the English, with their false modesty, like to call a 'flat'. This is the only way to obtain a *salon* bigger than a shoebox and the high ceilings which are *de rigueur* for grand parties. But a word of warning: forget about a concierge. There is no service culture in London, and you will find your private post thrown on to the communal hall table. Be wary of 'conversions': these are houses chopped up into flats, with bathrooms and bedrooms cut out of living rooms, resulting in a most offensive lack of architectural balance.

I myself was in search of a more Bohemian way of living. I saw my *séjour* in London as the chance to live more simply, to escape the pressing obligations that fell to me as part of *la bonne société* in Paris. I decided to abandon the grand staircase of my Haussmanien building in favour of a quaint front door opening on to a hall as cramped as a *chambre de bonne*.

I enlisted the help of an agent who found me a typical little worker's cottage, built for artisans in the 19th century. I cannot bring myself to tell you how much rent we pay; suffice it to say there are no longer any artisans living in the street. Instead, my neighbours are nearly all French, which is what you would expect in South Kensington. When we first meet, the question is always the same: *pétrolier ou banquier?* It's usually oil or the bank that brings us here!

The English prefer houses to flats because they like to 'have their own front door', though frankly I could do without the rain and dirt blowing into my house, and miss the exclusion zone of my entrance hall in rue du Tournon.

The English House Explained

Let me walk you through my own house in west London, and point out to you the peculiar features of the English home, of which they seem so inappropriately proud!

Like most London houses, mine stands indistinguishable from the others in a joined up line or 'terrace', hastily thrown up in the Victorian age. Up three steps to the front door, and you will notice a small potted bay tree chained to the railings (even in smart parts of town you cannot leave anything to chance, and every house is disfigured by a burglar alarm box). Through the front door, and you will be overcome by claustrophobia in the mean and narrow hall. Push open the door to the salon, where you might just have room, to borrow an English expression, to swing a cat. This is what they call a 'double reception room': a shrunken version of our own *double-living*, a peculiar corridor of a room with a window at each end. These 'sash' windows slide up and down and never fit properly, causing tremendous draughts which make it impossible to heat the room. They are also filthy, as they can only be reached for cleaning from the outside by a ladder.

The Basement Obsession

Follow me down the stairs, which you might think will lead to the cellar. Think again! Here is where the English live, like rats underground, hiding from the light, gazing up through prison bars on their grimy windows, to watch the legs of passers by. No expense has been spared in creating a luxury kitchen-dining room, but I ask you again, why would you choose to live like troglodytes? Needless to say, it is also the coldest room in the house: perfect perhaps for its original purpose of storing coal and wine, and for servants stoking the ovens, but not for middle class professionals hoping to enjoy gracious dinners.

This desire to live in the basement is part of the English nostalgia disease. Trapped in a sentimental fantasy of life below stairs, they pretend to be Victorian servants, and name their children accordingly. In the same spirit, they also pay a premium for humble mews houses converted from old stables on cobbled backstreets, so they can imagine they are coachmen to the gentry.

Shall We Go Upstairs?

If the basement of the English house is miserably cold with 'rising damp', the upper floor bedrooms will have you passing out in a hot summer. I spend the summers in France, but poor Pierre-Marie finds it quite unbearable, and cannot open the windows on account of the noise from aeroplanes (the whole of west London is blighted: only the English would allow flight paths over the smartest parts of town).

In the bathroom, don't expect to find twin basins: these are sneeringly branded 'his 'n' hers' and dismissed as continental affectations, as are bidets. Mercifully, the English are losing their unhygienic habit of carpeting bathroom floors, but the plumbing remains unfathomable, with no two showers operating in the same way. You cannot dry your hair in the bathroom – maybe that's why Englishwomen's hair is such a mess – because Nanny says it's too dangerous and won't allow a socket!

Expect to find a novelty lavatory seat in the cloakroom. The English like to express their personality by pressing autumn leaves into a Perspex toilet lid.

Snooper's Paradise

In French cities, the streets are a public theatre, where we engage with each other. But inside our apartments, we are private and invisible. In England, there is little street life, but everyone can stare into other people's homes and watch them.

So at dusk, I can walk down my road and look through the grimy sash windows to see vignettes of family life: the bored young mother feeding her child; the adolescent sprawling before the television;

the couple arguing in the kitchen. It is a paradise for snoopers, reminding us that this is the most spied-upon nation in Europe. More surveillance cameras are installed here than anyone else in Europe, accounting for 20 percent of the world's CCTV cameras.

Londoners are also keen on exchanging information at Neighbourhood Watch and Residents Association meetings, where the private householders get together to complain about the troublesome kids from the council estate. But it doesn't stop them being burgled!

Cleanliness

Two frightening pieces of information you should know about London: you are never more than three metres away from a rat, and the rubbish is only collected once or twice a week! You will obviously spot the correlation.

Even more frightening, perhaps, is the English failure to keep their homes clean. My friend in marketing tells me that Englishwomen are recognized as the sluts of Europe, with no feeling for housework, and this has certainly been my experience. Grubby, untidy rooms speak of no passion for order. I will never forget my childhood visit to an aunt by marriage, a retired professor who dressed like a tramp and spent her days wading through the Thames mud with a metal detector. Her house in Blackheath was unspeakably filthy.

Keeping a dirty home has regrettably become something of a badge of honour amongst the English, associated with cleverness. The writer Iris Murdoch was notoriously *bordelique* and when a visitor offered to clean the bath, Iris told her no, you don't need to do that. Oh yes I do, came the reply, I want to take a bath. There is now a popular TV show in which two cleaning ladies visit dirty homes and take the owners in hand. Can you imagine any Frenchwoman volunteering to endure such shame?

I confess it is a long time since I did my own house-work, but it is a question of knowing what is required and being firm with the servants, which seems to be quite beyond Englishwomen. They ingratiate themselves with the maid, rushing around to clean up before they come, then apologizing for the state of the house. This is a shame as cleaners become spoilt, making it harder for us Frenchwomen to demand the level of service we are used to.

My neighbour Bee made an inappropriate joke that it all came down to slavery being abolished so late in France. She said we still have the master-slave mentality that makes us treat our domestic staff badly. I said, if that means a better run house, so be it. In any case, the British only wanted to ban slavery to stop us getting ahead in the sugar industry. *De toute façon* I don't want my cleaner to be my friend. I'm French, remember.

Strangely, although they dislike housework, the English do sentimentalize it. Cath Kidston has made a fortune selling pretty ironing-board covers at inflated prices, recalling the well-ordered life of the 1950s housewife.

DIY

Though the English are not interested in keeping their houses clean, they are inordinately fond of altering them. In France, we spend Sundays at exhibitions. In England, they spend Sundays at the DIY superstore. Nothing excites them more than house plans, and I have spent interminable evenings at dinner parties where the conversation has struggled to rise above back extensions (Freudian enlargements jutting inappropriately into their back gardens: you rarely find a house in London that hasn't got one).

Once they have done their DIY, you will be forced to inspect the results. 'Shall we do the tour?' they'll ask, then lead you around, talking you through each 'improvement' in excruciating detail.

Interior Décor

The English may dress oddly, but their houses are all the same, at least in London.

Downstairs, the basement kitchen/diner will be sleekly modern in light colours, in a bid to counter-act the gloomy dungeon setting. The floor and units, will be pale wood with a black granite worktop as a nod to the dungeon. An ambitious cooking range hints deceitfully at culinary expertise. There may be a hob theatrically posed on an island unit, dominated by a huge steel fan-extractor.

Upstairs, by contrast, the modern theme is completely disregarded. The reception room is a worrying jumble of styles, stuffed full of antique chairs, rugs, books and bits of junk accumulated over twenty years that have been banished from the modernist dream room below. The English would say 'eclectic'; we would say a mess. They avoid symmetrical arrangements at all costs, offending our French sense of orderliness.

11

Gardening

'. . . to sit in the shade on a fine day and look upon
verdure is the most perfect refreshment.'

Jane Austen

The English prefer gardening to sex. Follow them around a garden centre, or better still, a specialist nursery. Feel that dowdy woman's excitement as she locates an obscure plant for her mixed border. Turning to her husband (both of them dressed like frights), she waves the pot at him and calls out its Latin name, as he nods and smiles his approval. It's the closest the English get to passion. I am told that the collective pulse of the nation was set racing by a TV presenter called Charlie Dimmock. To my eyes, she is a pleasant young woman who would benefit from make-up and grooming, but apparently her enthusiasm for horticulture was enough to promote her to the status of a sex symbol.

In France, we know what makes a good garden. Gravel, single specimen shrubs, and bright neat pots of geraniums. A clipped hedge and a plain green trellis, stark against a white wall. No mess.

In contrast, the English garden is an undisciplined, unruly thing, tumbling about in messy profusion. Anarchic herbaceous borders make a virtue of randomness. They bend over backwards to be casual.

This shows how we French have kept gardens in their place: formal, man-made places that speak of civilization. We have our well-ordered *parterres* and *potagers*, while the English go mad in a romantic, gothic wilderness.

The Garden Shed

In the world of the English gardener, enormous importance is accorded to the room where they keep their tools. The Garden Shed is the place where Englishmen want to be. Cut off from the world is how it feels, though in reality it's just a short shuffle in slippers and pyjamas from the back door.

It started out as a simple hut, where the retired Englishman could sit with his cup of tea, listen to his wireless and inspect his seedlings. Then came lighting, heating, wireless internet connections, and all of a sudden, it's the Home Office, and he has the perfect excuse to spend all day there. Take out a sandwich, speak to no one, and dream of being Scott of the Antarctic*.

Garden sheds are often the setting for sex scenes in books and films, and have become an important selling point for every house. Offering the chance to be alone, they bring out the Greta Garbo in every Englishman.

The Chelsea Flower Show

My first year in London, I thought I would look in on the Chelsea Flower Show, as it is close to where I live. I was laughed away at the gate: tickets had been sold out weeks before. Pink-cheeked women up from the country marched past me, tweed skirts, sensible anoraks, ferocious knowledge of botany displayed in snippets of overheard conversation. I have never seen English people so passionately aroused. There were plenty of people in suits, too: I learned that an invitation to the Chelsea Flower Show is one of the most sought-after forms of corporate entertainment.

The following year, I bought a ticket and found myself swept along in the most monstrous crowds,

---

*The future of the Antarctic hut from which explorer Captain Scott walked to his death has been the subject of impassioned debate. It is in many ways the ultimate garden shed.

doing what the English like doing best (after gardening): queuing. Along the main line of gardens, there
was a choice of two queues, 'fast' or 'slow', depend-
ing on how long you wish to linger in front of each
display. Dutiful ranks of gardeners snake round in
regulated lines. I do not queue for anything, so
limited myself to the gardens you get to see by
pushing your way to the front. Some of them were
downright scruffy. I fail to see the attraction of a rusty
old gate and plants spilling out of battered old metal
buckets! This was supposed to be Provençal in theme,
though I can assure you I would never tolerate that
mess in my own garden, and nor would any of my
neighbours in the Luberon.

After being jostled down a Disney-esque high
street of shops selling garden knick-knacks, Marie-
Chantal and I agreed over a glass of Veuve Cliquot
that we much preferred the Art du Jardin exhibition
in the bois de Boulogne. Far more restrained with just
a handful of show gardens: Yves St Laurent, Vogue,
names synonymous with *le luxe français*, using
pillars and ribbons with most elegant results. Plus
you can park and take home pots of scented geraniums, instead of being ushered around as if in a zoo
and only able to buy placemats depicting garden
scenes.

Watch Your Head

The British are sentimental about trees, and refuse to restrain them the way we do, by pollarding the branches to make neat mutated forms. Consequently, you will often have to step off the pavement to avoid low-hanging branches, and may find yourself on the top deck of a bus, terrified by the sound of branches crashing into the vehicle.

Garden Snobbery

Like everything in England, gardening is subject to class divisions. So although you might think a rose is just a rose, that would be a grave error. Old roses are upper class, modern roses common; small flowered clematis are upper class, large flowered clematis are common. Hostas upper class, dahlias common. Latin plant name, good, English plant name common.

This snobbery extends to TV gardening shows. On the upper-class side, we have Monty Don, a lanky poet and gentleman in the sensitive Vita Sackville-West tradition. And weighing in for the common man is little Alan Titchmarsh, all dirty innuendo and broad winks for his audience of old ladies: 'Shall I tell you the Latin name of this plant? It's I don't-know-and-I-don't-give-a-damn.'

My neighbour Bee tells me of similar snobberies concerning allotments in London. In France, of course, allotments are strictly for the poor who supplement their income by growing vegetables. In England, everyone wants a go. On Bee's allotment patch, the plots were allocated evenly between well-off private householders and council tenants, resulting in class warfare. The bourgeoisie feared the organic status of their raddichio might be compromised by the massive, chemically enhanced crops of their proletarian neighbours.

Fashion Victims

Particularly in smaller town gardens, the English are prone to becoming fashion victims. Inspired by TV programmes, they install ill-advised wooden decks that become slimey and slippery beneath the London rain (do they imagine they are in the Deep South, smoking their pipes on rocking chairs?) Feng Shui gardens show a half-hearted nod to spirituality, Japanese Zen gardens import gravel and bamboo, reminiscent of our own French gardens which is perhaps why the English have now gone off them.

Nostalgie de la boure

The green-fingered English may flirt with modern ideas, but at the heart of their gardening passion lies the dream of the past. The great country house, with its attendant acres of high-maintenance gardens and two-metre-deep beds. Or its humble equivalent, the jumbled up cottage garden, depicted on greetings cards, where sweet peas and strawberries tumble over roses and daisies.

With what agonizing precision the English seek to create this mess! Pierre-Marie likes to relax by gardening at the weekends, and was using a ruler to plant out a neat row of begonias one day when Bee dropped round to brag, in that falsely self-deprecating way, about her son's exam results.

'God, you're so French, Pierre-Marie,' she said, 'can't you just make it a bit more *random*.'

By which she means that confusing arrangement she has, with her untrimmed honeysuckle hanging over our wall, and the seeds from her myosotis lodging in our brickwork. I ask you, what's wrong with the one-bulb-one-pot logic that makes our back garden the neatest in the street? (I know, because I can see them all from my bathroom window, thanks to the goldfish bowl design of London homes.)

It all comes down to the industrial revolution. The English scarred their landscape with monstrous development (do take a trip to the North country to see the full horror), then compensated by putting in romantic, studiedly 'naturalistic' gardens by Capability Brown.

We never went through that cycle, which explains why we've always known how to keep gardens in their place. Our country house in Brittany is surrounded by an efficient ring of cement to keep down weeds, then a neat *parc* that can be efficiently mown by the gardener on his tractor. Correct and manageable. The time the English spend tending their rose bushes, we spend tending our *esprit*. They could learn a lot from us!

12

The Countryside

'Don't have too much faith in the idea that the
countryside is good for you. Nature detests us . . .'
Alfred de Vigny

The English have an absurdly romantic view of
the countryside. They dream of leaving behind
everything that is *dynamique* to go and vegetate in an
isolated cottage.*

Can you imagine *choosing* to lock yourself away
from the world to dig potatoes, in a routine where the
high point of the day is walking out to post a letter?
This is what they want! Pottering around in damp
obscurity with no reason to wear decent clothes, just
DIY and TV, mending the thatched roof before
settling down with a nice cup of tea to watch *Deal or
No Deal*.

*This perversion is a hangover of the industrial revolution, when
the English devastated their landscape. While our writers
pointed out the bleak reality of country life, English writers gave
it the rosy sheen of paradise lost.

And because England is so cramped and running out of old houses, they are pouring into France to buy up ours! My dear friend the Ambassador held a seminar on this phenomenon: we can only conclude that the English are emotionally damaged and unable to connect with civilized society, preferring to live a half-life in old jogging pants with only their pets for company.

A Place in the Country

As a staging post to complete rural exile, those who can afford to it will buy a 'weekend place'. The assumption is that if it wasn't for work, they would live here all the time. *Quelle idée!*

Many Parisians have second homes, but it is unthinkable for us to forego the city. When I lived in Paris, I took pleasure in visiting the country for a weekend of fresh air, the joys of simple food with simple people, but two days is enough. After that you become lazy and depressed, so my rule was always to have the car packed and ready to return by *l'heure du goûter* at four o'clock on Sunday afternoon.

And let us be clear, a Parisian would never try to pass himself off as a provincial. Indeed, he would be most insulted if someone mistook him for a local. Yet the weekending London banker is flattered if someone thinks he lives full time in Gloucestershire, and invests in an entire wardrobe in order to look the part: waxed coat, country casuals, Wellington boots that preferably leave muddy traces in the car. Everything must look old and faded, as if it has been in the family for generations. And here we come to the essential difference: the English countrydweller is a gentleman in tweeds*, where the French country-dweller is a clog-wearing *paysan*.

Here are some English show business personalities who pretend to be country gentlefolk: Madonna's husband Guy Ritchie, retired 'Brit pop' singer Alex James, Kate Moss, actress Elizabeth Hurley.

Although I am a little naughty about the English enthusiasm for the countryside, I love nothing better than being invited away for a weekend. This is when you get to see the English at their most relaxed, when they drop their guard, and might even say something they mean!

A Country Weekend

In Paris, a weekend cottage must be within two hours' drive. Unfortunately, a two-hour drive from

---

*This is historical: our aristocrats left their county estates to be with the king at court, whereas the English ruling class remained at their country seats.

London will barely take you out of the suburbs, so the English will sit patiently on jammed motorways, peering into each other's cars, grazing on crisps and sandwiches and Maltesers. After the massive road junction that is south-east England thins out there will be a further two hours through the dark and the rain before you arrive. The house will be as difficult to find as possible; they lay great store in being hidden away at the bottom of an obscure muddy lane. Whereas we prefer a prominent location, so everyone can admire the *jolie façade* from a main road giving easy access.

What to Pack

From our many years' experience of country weekends, I would strongly advise you to ensure your *valise* contains the following:

1. Warm Clothes. Even the wealthy English are mean about heating their houses, and suffering in three layers of sweaters is supposed to be all part of the 'fun', though I fail to see where the fun is to be found in bedroom windows with ice *on the inside*.

2. An Electric Blanket, see above.

3 Waxed Country-Style Coat that must appear old and battered. With their mixed-up snobbery, the

English will consider you vulgar if your clothes look new. It's all part of their longing to be eccentric aristocrats, although they are irredeemably middle class (see Chapter 27, on Class). You won't need to take anything elegant: country weekenders dress down, unlike full-time country English who put on long dresses and jewellery for dinner parties to try to pretend they don't miss the city.

4. Emergency Food Supplies. English people take slabs of their chocolate-style confectionery to fill up, in case the food is really bad. I always pack some unsalted nuts and dried fruit, *au cas ou*.

5. Johnnie Boden Moleskin Skirt, 'fun tank top' and 'good mood tee' T-shirt embroiderd with garish flowers and sequins. Go on, you might as well let your habitual good taste slip and go native with English country wear – they won't realize you're making fun of them!

6. Bottles of Wine and Board Games. 'Getting away from it all' means no TV and playing old fashioned games, recreating their own childhoods. Except now they have to play Monopoly washed down with several glasses of chardonnay.

7. Aspirin. The country weekend is another excuse for excessive drinking, and you'll find your glass is

permanently topped up. The next morning you'll need to take medication before going down for the egg and bacon.

8. Money. In France, *une invitation, c'est une invitation* and we don't expect our guests to fund their stay. The stingy English, incapable of cooking, are likely to take you to the pub at every opportunity, where you will feel obliged to pay for them.

The Long Muddy Walk

After the discomfort of a cold bedroom and indigestible food comes the unavoidable centrepiece of the English country weekend: the long muddy walk. Where we might drive to a tennis court, or to the market, or drop in for *un crème* at an agreeable café, the English will pull on their boots and head out 'to walk off our breakfast' over wretchedly unmade tracks. At some point, it might be discussed whether one should take the 'long or the short route', but be warned: even the short is far too long. Ideally, the walk will include climbing over stiles and barbed wire fences and marching across people's back gardens, enforcing the 'right to ramble' law that allows English people to trespass on private property in a way we would never tolerate.

The worse the weather, the more they enjoy it, though if the sun should come out, they will strip off layers of coats and jumpers and tie them round their waist in a bulky confusion. During the walk, you will fall into small groups and make fatuous conversation, though I always find the pointlessness of the exercise throws me into an existentialist gloom and I am incapable of small talk. Then a pub called something like the Wily Fox and Gherkin comes into view. 'Lunchtime!' says your host, reminding you that your delicate physical balance is about to be further challenged by pints of warm beer and food that is best described by that appropriate English expression 'hit and miss'.

The Country Pub

The pub has no sense of territory. You could be in Yorkshire, Wales, Sussex or Mayfair: there is no clue from the décor or the food, which is entirely random and usually served by foreign staff. I have eaten 'oysters in beer batter and Thai sauce' on the North York Moors, 'minted lamb stew with roll' in Scotland (note the singular 'roll', don't you dare ask for any more bread) and *tapas* and Catalan stew in a Welsh mining village. A microwaved jacket potato, hot in the middle, cold outside, with canned tuna fish and 'salad garnish' of a lettuce leaf and half an unripe tomato remains a national staple.

As for the décor, it usually goes as follows: 'character' low beams from which knick-knacks dangle, non-matching chairs and stools, and insufficient numbers of small tables from which you are supposed to eat, so you'll end up balancing your plate on your lap. You may find the only reasonable sized table is occupied by two old people sitting over half a pint of beer. In this case, lengthy negotiations will ensue, resulting in them being shuffled off to another seat, while your party takes over the table, feeling guilty.

When we have lunch at a café in France, we sit down and the waiter comes to take our order. This is too straightforward for the English, who prefer a free-for-all scrum. First there is the great fuss over who is paying for the beer, and a lot of jostling goes on between the men about who's going to 'get them in'. It's immaterial as honour will not be satisfied until everyone has 'bought their round', which goes to explain their staggering capacity for drink.

Once everyone has their pint, or their glass of wine (the usual measure is a third of a bottle), your thoughts will anxiously turn to food. I have learned the best policy is to assume the only thing on offer will be a bag of prawn cocktail flavour crisps, and then you will not be disappointed (and if you are wise, you will have your *au cas ou* fruit and unsalted nuts in your bag).

Ordering food begins with someone battling their way up to the bar again and asking for some menus. There won't be enough to go round, so you'll have to take it in turns to read, or have someone shout across to you. Like the drinks, the food is 'pay as you go', so everyone will have to pull out their wallets ('buying your round' never extends to food) and queue at the far end of the bar where a young girl will write down each order as if it's the first time she's ever done it. You then make your way back to stand in your group, restlessly looking around the room in case a table should become available. With luck you may end up sitting together by the time the food comes out, one plate at a time, hot or not. *Franchement,* you'd be better off at home.

Fox-hunting

The ban on fox-hunting had a peculiar effect on the luke-warm English. They actually took to the streets to demonstrate, just like proper *citoyens*. Naturally the cause involved animals, though oddly, it was the right to have them viciously torn apart that they were defending, and not the right to have them treated like sentient beings.*

Fortunately the law has been widely disregarded and the 'pink' (by which they mean red) coats of the tally-ho hunters remain one of the few smart items in the English wardrobe. The red coats can now be seen around Pau in south-western France, where English exiles have set up a hunt in the land of the free where we do not care to restrict the life of the individual by petty regulation. (Even if it was banned, we would just do what we always do: ignore the law, and carry on as we please.)

Shooting is still permitted and pheasants almost too heavy to fly are pulverized on corporate days out by city and suburban types playing at being country gentlemen.

Mais quand même!

There are a few positive points about being in the country:

---

*Why a fox should be treated so differently from a dog, I really don't know, but who am I to judge? I am merely a French *philosophe de dimanche* engaged in understanding the human condition, and for whom the life of the animal is entirely secondary.

You may meet *un vrai gentleman* (and it's easier to get to know people in the country);

The country is useful as a place to recuperate from cosmetic surgery;

You will feel even slimmer in the English countryside than you do in their cities: those pub lunches certainly take their toll on the countrywoman's figure!

13

The Weather

'Nothing can distract the imagination from the depression the climate creates, and the most intrepid curiosity will not resist the pitiless monotony that presides over everyday life in this temple of boredom.'

Astolphe de Custine, Courses en Angleterre et en Écosse 1830

You might think that global warming would be a good thing for the miserable English weather. Summer heat waves bring discomfort to homes and transport designed for a moderate climate. Winters no longer offer snow, merely a mild dampness that sends them running for the English sun-ray lamps to dispel their Seasonal Affected Disorder. Whatever the season, you know you'd feel better in France.

The Rain

English rain deserves its reputation. A constant grey companion, it drizzles on and off, but never with sufficient vigour to fill the reservoirs or even to merit the use of an umbrella. As if in sympathy with the incontinent skies, the underground water pipes all leak, turning the country into a giant marsh – but one in a continual state of drought.

I'll overlook the winter rain – after all, the weather in Paris is not so good at this time. But picture a typical day in May, when you might have been lunching on a terrace in the Palais Royal, or sitting in the sunshine in Roland Garros. Instead, you are pulling on a mac and battling down the high street, as the wind inverts your umbrella and blows the litter up in your face. It is impossible to look good in your spring wardrobe in such conditions.

Smiling TV weather girls make jokes about naughty 'bits and pieces' of rain and reassure viewers that it will be good for the garden. *On s'en fout!**. Who cares about the garden! If people are a product of their climate, then the deep Russian thinkers have intellects fuelled by vodka and icy winters, the laissez-faire West Indians are relaxed by the sun, the complicated French are a beguiling blend of Mediterranean heat and winter snow. And the English?

*Translator's note: delivered with the inimitable Gallic scowl, '*On s'en fout*' gives full expression to its meaning of 'we couldn't care less'. Also found in the politer version '*On s'en fiche*'.

Phlegmatic in the face of dampness, they shrug their shoulders and laugh about it. 'Good old English weather!' they will say to each other, huddled in towels beneath an umbrella on a beach, or wrestling with the windbreak*. Why do you always complain about the weather? I often ask them, after yet another lengthy grumble about the wind/rain/sleet. They always look really surprised. Oh no, they say, we're not complaining, we are just talking about it.

Here are my *astuces* for when you get depressed by the English weather.

* Watch a French film like Les Choses d'Été to remind you how the sun always shines in France.
* Take a beauty treatment in a spa.
* Take a plane to a country with a better climate. You soon get hooked on the British passion for the 'mini-break' when you see what they have to put up with at home.

The Sun

The English in the rain are bad enough, with their macs and rainhats and irritatingly cheerful stoicism.

*Only the English would sell a piece of equipment to keep the wind off sunbathers. If the wind is howling over the beach, maybe it's just not sunbathing weather?

But just wait until the sun shines. It's a horrible sight. Every patch of public grass will be occupied by sunbathers, stripped to the skin: trousers rolled up, bare chests, skirts pulled up for maximum exposure. At weekends, they might even wear bikinis and trunks, regardless of their physique. It makes me homesick for those *pelouse interdite* signs and whistle-blowing *gardiens* who keep our Paris parks fit for their purpose; elegant promenades and people watching – by which I mean watching people with their clothes on, not sprawled half naked with six cans of beer and a pile of sandwiches.

Failure to Dress for Weather

There is no such thing as bad weather, only unsuitable clothing. I do wish the English would heed this dictum and dress to suit their climate. How often have I seen crowds huddled outside the metro, no coats, no umbrellas, caught out by the downpour outside even though rain was forecast all week? In the countryside, where we French have adopted *le style anglais* in immaculate new Barbours and green rubber boots, the English are more likely to be found wearing inadequate flimsy clothes and trainers.

I have not been to the North country, but Pierre-Marie reported with disbelief a business trip to Leeds where he saw girls in short skirts, T-shirts and bare legs walking down the street on a bleak winter's afternoon. Even in the south, they are careless of the cold. When I went on a guided walking tour of Jack the Ripper's *quartier* of east London one day in October (so much to learn, I warmly recommend walking tours, such a refreshing contrast to one's indoor hobbies*) a woman approached me to ask me if I was French. How did you know? I asked.

'I am French too,' she said, 'and we are the only two people who are wearing a coat.'

English mothers are as negligent with their children as they are with themselves. They never dress them in snug woollen balaclavas like we do, and I have seen small babies kicking *bare* feet in the pram. I once approached a stranger in the street to warn her that her baby would catch a cold, but she replied in very uncivil terms to the effect that we French were over-zealous about our health and comfort!

---

*Besides *scrapbooking*, I also paint Ukrainian eggs and make jewellery which I sell on a private basis through sales in friends' homes. Don't bother inviting Englishwomen to these events; they are notoriously unwilling to spend money supporting their sisters.

14

The English and Their Health

'Take your medicaments with you, and if you're not
well, go back to France. Health care in England is very
expensive and sometimes bizarre.'
*Advice for expatriates to England on the HEC website.**

One of the things the English really hate us for is
being so healthy. 'It's not fair,' they complain,
hand in the crisp packet, 'you drink all that wine,
smoke, eat nothing but fattened goose liver, and you
still get to wear a size eight dress until you're a
hundred and fifty.'

To which I reply, 'Why don't you just put down that
packet of fudge fingers and start to take your health
seriously?'

But they just can't. Which is possibly as well when
you look at the health care offered by this very rich
nation.

My advice to anyone French at the first symptom

*Translator's note: 'HEC' is a top Paris business school, a *grande
école.*

137

of any ailment is: get on the Eurostar to see your specialist. It's as comfortable as a British ambulance and much faster. And no one in France is going to think you a hypochondriac.

How Are You?

Even people you don't know will greet you with the question, 'How are you?' There is only one acceptable reply, and that is, 'I'm fine, thanks.' There are no exceptions to this rule. You can be lying in hospital after major surgery, or crippled by a debilitating disease, but still you must insist that you are 'fine'. This is to demonstrate your courage and insouciance in the face of adversity, whereas we French are not afraid to admit that *'C'est catastrophique.'*

Being 'fine' must also extend to your mental state. Hours after his wife had died, an English friend of mine went for a coffee at the café opposite the hospital where he had become a regular.

'How are you, sir?' asked the owner, as he always did.

'Oh, I'm fine, thanks,' said my friend.

What else should he say? This is called having a 'stiff upper lip', which does not translate into French, as it means not crying and never showing one's emotions. The English are very proud of it.

Medical Vocabulary

Ill at ease with their bodies at the best of times, the English become rigid with denial when something goes wrong. This denial involves never giving any illness its proper name.

Here are their woefully vague translations of some common afflictions:

une gastro-enterite	a bit of a tummy upset
une rhinopharyngite	a cold
une angine	sore throat
une otite	ear ache, 'my ears hurt'
une crise de foie	indigestion
40 degrés de fièvre	a temperature (never specified)

The terms are always as non-specific as possible, and delivered with an nonchalant shrug to imply that we French are hypochondriacs because we dare to confront the enemy and make a precise medical diagnosis, instead of limply claiming to be 'a bit under the weather'.

Doctor Who?

In France, we behave like adults, and make our own decisions about which doctor to consult. Forget that in England, unless you are extremely rich. Even those with private health insurance are allowed to see just one general practitioner, and any referrals must go through him! This is accepted with child-like obedience – the less fuss made, the better, and don't expect to be given custody of your own X-rays. These will be passed secretively around, and considered too precious to remain in your care – it's only your body after all!

Seeing a Doctor

As I've said, it will be quicker to go to France. You have to ring at set times, you cannot book appointments in advance, and must take whatever time you are offered by a secretary who is the closest you will find to a French *fonctionnaire* in terms of inflexibility. The UK may be entirely centred around the modern Anglo-Saxon invention that is 'the consumer', but when it comes to the health system, you could be in the Third World.

Pierre-Marie has a private health plan as part of his 'package'*, so the first thing I did was ring round to organize my usual basic health appointments (*dermatologue, gynécologue, kinesthérapeute,*

---

*Another greedy Anglo-Saxon term, a gift-wrapped parcel of employee rewards and incentives.

psychologue). Imagine my surprise when I was told that these appointments would not be honoured by my insurance. What do you pay for then, I asked? It appears all I qualify for is a better room if I ever have non-elective surgery.

As for getting a doctor to visit you at home, you could die first. My dear friend almost did when he rang his surgery and said he had a 'bit of a sore throat' and couldn't make it into the surgery. They told him to keep warm and drink Lemsip. He eventually realized things weren't getting any better and drove himself into hospital, where he was admitted to intensive care with pneumonia and one-and-a-half lungs entirely full of liquid. I told him afterwards about 'SOS Médecins'*. He thought I was 'having a laugh' and couldn't believe such a thing possible.

Dentistry

'English teeth' is an evocative term, which brings to mind medieval pictures of brown and crooked teeth. It is almost impossible to obtain free dental care, and

*Translator's note: one of the miracles of the French social system, which has English expats weeping with gratitude. You ring for a doctor who comes to your house within the hour, and all for the price of a round in the pub which is then reimbursed by the state.

private dentists charge such high prices that it is cheaper for me to buy a first-class Eurostar ticket for a consultation in Paris. However, following Pierre-Marie's remarks about how often I seemed to be deserting him for the pleasures of Paris, I have tried to shift my focus back to England, and through the pages of *Ici Londres* magazine have now found a French *cabinet dentaire* based in London.

Accident and Emergency (Pray You Don't Have One)

If you have an accident in England, make sure it's not on Friday or Saturday night. I had to accompany Pierre-Marie to the hospital once when he cut himself on an oyster knife. It was most unfortunate: the oysters had been ordered from Waitrose, the knife obtained with some difficulty, and after all the evening was ruined. We sat in our *tenue de ville* for *four hours* watching a parade of drunks lurch in, interspersed with stoic respectable citizens, whose patience bordered on the imbecilic. I whispered to Pierre-Marie that it would not be tolerated in France, we would storm the consulting room. Worst of all, when we were eventually seen by a doctor, he pronounced Pierre-Marie's wound 'very superficial' and refused to give any treatment beyond a perfunctory bandage!

Other dates to avoid 'A & E'* are 5 November, when the English have their barbarous 'Bonfire Night' to celebrate Guy Fawkes' plot to blow up the Houses of Parliament. Instead of attending official firework displays, as we do on Bastille Day (in mid-summer, the proper season for outdoor parties), the English set fire to cones of gunpowder in their back gardens, resulting in countless injuries.

The English 'Pharmacy'

I use the *guillemets* or 'inverted commas' judiciously. Consider the glory of the French pharmacy. Six on every high street, clearly signalled by the illuminated sign of the green cross. Each with that intoxicating perfume, a heady blend of *médicaments* and luxury face creams. Here reigns the atmosphere of a private health clinic, with white uniformed pharmacists ready to administer your list of six medicines (naturally we would not consult a doctor who prescribed any less).

Now, let me show you an English pharmacy. It's called Boots and it's a cut-price general store. You walk in to find sandwiches, films, umbrellas,

*'Accident and Emergency,' which we call *Urgences*, though God forbid you ever have anything truly *urgent*.

hair-dryers. Beauty care and vitamin pills follow, with signs screaming at you to buy three for the price of two. You *help yourself* to medicines right off the shelf. Has no one told them how dangerous it is to self-administer paracetamol? A French pharmacy would never sell you more than one packet. At the far end, hidden from view, is a small counter where they make up the prescriptions (rarely more than two items). Rather than serve you right away, they'll send you off for fifteen minutes so you can spend more money in the shop. Not so much a medical centre, more a superstore.

Suppositories

Be prepared for jokes about this most efficient method of administering medicine: the puerile English sense of humour again, combined with scientific ignorance. They'll tell you holiday tales of French doctors suggesting suppositories, 'but I said to him, no, it's my *throat* that's the problem . . .'

The Gynaecologist

The English do not have gynaecologists, they have Well Women Clinics or Family Planning Centres which sound less frightening to them. This is hardly

surprising since sex and medical terminology are subjects best not spoken of. They are richly amused by
our programme of post-natal *rééducation périnéale.**
The idea that you should take action to prevent prob-
lems with your *vie intime* is considered both hilarious
and mad.

*Translator's note: after childbirth, French women are entitled
to six free sessions with a physiotherapist to 're-educate' their
perineum, involving manual and electronic monitoring of the
strength of the vaginal contractions.

15

The Family

'The most ancient of all societies, and the only natural
one, is that of the family.'

Jean-Jacques Rousseau, Du Contrat Social

The English make an enormous fuss about having a baby, and like to tell everyone how it has changed their life. They put 'Baby on Board' stickers in their car windows as a badge of honour. Emasculated new fathers sit in the back seat, tending to Baby, or carrying him around in a little sling. They live in terror of contravening Health and Safety rules and provoking a cot death.

This desperation springs from a complete lack of infrastructure. As the African proverb reminds us, it takes a village to raise a child, but there is little sense of collective responsibility for bringing up little Johnny. He is stuck within his nuclear family, God help him, always assuming he is not born to a single teenage mother (of whom there are more in England than anywhere in Europe).

The Family

How different from our own flourishing society, underpinned by the extended family. I have a photograph on my wall, taken at our family house in Brittany when my children were very young. Ten little cousins sitting happily around the table eating *fruits de mer*, with their parents, aunts, uncles. You don't get that in England, and I've no idea how they manage in the summer, since grandparents *never* invite their grandchildren to stay. This is because they are too busy gardening or spending their children's inheritance to remember their family obligations.

Here are some tips I can share with you about English parenting:

Don't expect an English child to eat proper food. Even 'foodie' parents will dish out fish-fingers for the kids before preparing their own feast. One mother stopped me when I was serving her child a simple pasta dish, with the words 'He's not a sauce person'. I never heard anything so ridiculous.

Because of their faddy eating habits, English children have no discipline and can never sit round a table with adults.

English children eat dinner at five o'clock so it is 'out of the way', freeing them up to snack through the rest of the evening.

English parents have a child shoe fetish and insist on getting their kids' feet measured for width by 'trained' shop assistants: a waste of time since the minute they grow up the girls will be cramming their toes into stilettos.

At children's parties, you are supposed to provide a full meal of sandwiches, sausage rolls, etc., and not just the little *goûter* that we consider appropriate for 4 p.m. You must also spend a forture on entertainers and send every little guest home with a bagful of presents.

Don't sit next to an English child on an aeroplane, they are loud and badly behaved.

English children are badly brought up and will never say the equivalent of '*Bonjour madame*' to an adult. Instead it's just an offhand 'Hi'.

Stay-at-Home English Mothers

There are two sorts of *mères au foyer*: 'yummy mummies' who look like well-groomed *Parisiennes*, and drudges, who don't.

The yummy mummy is materialistic and boastful, but at least she is light-hearted. Her basic position is 'Only a fool would choose to go out to work; I am quite happy to live off my successful husband in an ironic post-feminist take on the 1950s housewife.'* She may start a home business, selling household linen or expensive baby clothes.

More frightening is the drudge in anorak and sensible shoes, bowed over her children's homework, all sense of self forgotten as she channels her ambition into her offspring. As often in this money-driven nation, it is usually the husband's salary that decides whether his wife falls into the yummy or drudge category.

English mothers spend too much time worrying about their role, starting in pregnancy, when they force their husbands to attend pointless breathing classes with them.

In France when it comes to the birth we check into a *clinique* for a comfortable epidural and then stay in for a week's bed rest. The English prefer to beat themselves up in a Protestant lather about wanting to conquer the pain with primitive gas and air, and rush home the moment the child is born. And whereas we are sensible enough to have *bébé* taken care of while we sleep, they lie awake, wild-eyed, trying to clamp the baby on to their breast 'because

*People have referred to me as a yummy mummy, a title I reject. I am a Sciences Po graduate with a distinguished career that has been on hold since I elected to devote myself to studying English behaviour.

if he's given a bottle, he'll never latch on' and will suffer immunity deficiency. Such nonsense, and frankly these women would do well to think of themselves in all this. Do they really want to ruin their figure and their wardrobe by encouraging distended, leaky breasts?

Once out of hospital, the yummy mummy will loudly endorse the state of grace that is middle-class English parenthood. She will wheel the child around department stores, clipping everyone's heels with her huge triangular buggy and talking to him loudly about what she is intending to buy for his nursery. On Saturdays, the proud father will join the shopping expedition, so they can shout to each other in the lift about whether the child has dropped its juice and what style of blinds would be best for the nanny's room.

If only they could acquire some French discretion! We accept that children are part of life, joyfully embraced, but not an excuse to behave like a loud-mouthed evangelist!

I should add that English mothers who go out to work are less prone to the above – they retain a better sense of balance and, dare I say it, a more *French* approach to childrearing.

Children's Place in Society

Individually, the English love their children. Collectively, they can't stand them.

To see the low esteem in which children are held, try taking your family to an English pub. Dogs may be welcome, but children most definitely are not. You will be barred entry, or ushered into the 'family room', a brightly lit annexe with indestructible plastic furniture that will make you wish you'd stayed at home. I have seen a man turned away for carrying a newborn baby asleep in a sling. Had he put it on a lead and pretended it was a puppy, he would have been admitted.

Even when booking bed and breakfast accommodation for a tour of the West Country, I had trouble securing rooms for children under fourteen. I was told 'they might disturb the other guests'. *Incroyable*. Of course I told them that was *hors de question*: my children were French and therefore knew how to behave, but also that I would not entertain the idea of booking into an establishment that treated junior *citoyens* like criminals. I then went on to say that no wonder English children were so awful, when people like him *expected* them to be a nuisance, and that it was people like him who gave English hosts their bad reputation and I would be advising all my friends to boycott his establishment. I regret to say he then launched into an ugly xenophobic attack along the lines that I was 'typical French' and the last thing he'd want would be me finding fault with his full English breakfast.

16

Education

'England – where they eat anything, anytime, and
where girls aged 12–60 dress like peepshow *danseuses*.'
*Anonymous French blogger, lamenting the inadequacies of
English education.*

The French word *éducation* translates quite differently into English. For us, it means all aspects of raising a child: from table manners and correct forms of address, to learning *le catéchisme* and how to dance *le rock*. And – dare I say it – respecting one's elders.

For the English, it just means school, as in the ill-mannered song 'We don't need no education'.

English Schools

The best thing about coming to live in England is realizing how lucky we are to be French! Not least in terms of education. At home, we send our child to the local school, which of course is funded by the state.

In a brilliant feat of coordination, every child will be following the same lesson in a given week all over the country. So democratic and rational. Thirty in a class, iron discipline, a zero tolerance policy for miscreants, and if a child hasn't learned the lessons by the end of the year, no problem, he can do it again. Thirty-eight percent of French schoolchildren repeat a school year at some point.

In contrast, English parents are bowed down by anxiety about 'finding a school' for their child, and wear a worried expression from conception until the child's eighteenth birthday, which is very ageing. It also makes them intolerably dull. How often have my eyes glazed over at parties, when they start talking about it! 'Excuse me for interrupting, but I believe you were with Miss Jenny at St Dunstans. Can we talk? We have some important decisions to take . . .' Then off they go, hunched in anxious consultation. Such poor manners.

Webcams in Nursery Schools!

So paranoid are the English about their children that many private nursery schools have installed cameras. This enables worried English parents to spend their days at the office gazing at images of their child weeping over his organic lunch-box. How very unlike our *halte-garderies** where proper discipline is instilled from the earliest age and we will not tolerate weakness masquerading as 'separation anxiety'.

'The Right School'

The English will go to any lengths to get their children into 'the right school'. Putting an unborn child on a waiting list, buying an overpriced house to be in the correct catchment area, hypocritically attending church to pass off as Christians for a faith school. Then they will *pay* for private schools. In France, boarding schools are only for problem children; nobody would choose to send their child *en pension*, it's like putting an animal in a zoo. Yet here, they compete for the privilege, inspired by dim memories of the British Empire, when young men were raised in barbaric conditions at public school before being sent off to govern primitive lands. (My knowledge of psychology tells me it is because the parents themselves suffered cold showers and dormitory cruelty that they instinctively wish to inflict the same on their children.)

---

*Translator's note: *halte-garderies* are rather frightening state nurseries, where French parents are encouraged to leave their babies to get them institutionalized from the earliest age.

Private schools (also known as public schools) are an affront to British democracy. True, we have exclusivity in France, with top jobs going to the 120 annual graduates of the top university Ecole Nationale d'Administration*). But every one of those will have come through a state school. Compare this to Britain, where 7 percent of children attend private school, yet 70 percent of barristers, 54 percent of the media and 42 percent of government/shadow ministers were privately educated. So much for the 'new ladders of social mobility' promised by the last government!

School Uniform

My neighbour Bee is a great defender of school uniform. Her children go out every morning in their silly blazers and caps. She says it makes 'everyone equal' though of course the opposite is true, since everyone knows by their uniform who goes to which school, and therefore where they stand socially. How we give thanks for our own *égalité*, where French children wear what they like to school, instinctively choosing stylish yet practical clothes that are entirely classless.

*Fortunately, my husband is an *ancien élève*.

The problem of school uniform – aside from the unnecessary expense of running parallel wardrobes – is that English teenagers waste a lot of time attempting to circumvent the rules. So you get the skirt rolled up at the waist, the *mauvais garçon* knotting of the tie, the hooker tights, pathetic cries for attention from rebels without a cause. The famously eccentric British fashion sense is a result of this kicking against the boundaries; I can only assume the Brit designers currently directing our French fashion houses 'had school uniform issues', as the English would say.

My son Pierre-Edouard was mercilessly teased one day by Bee's son Jez* for wearing a well cut pair of Cyrillus trousers, peach summer shoes and an apricot sweater that just happened to match his father's Sunday outfit.

'It's gay to look like your parents,' said Jez. (I should explain that 'gay' is used by the young to describe anything they don't like; it has nothing to do with sexual orientation.) I found this remark interesting. Since Jez has to spend all week in a blazer, shirt and tie, like a miniature version of his father, he feels obliged to dress like a tramp or a rock

*Abbreviation of Jeremy. Bee's daughter is called PJ, but I have not worked out what that is short for.

star at the weekend, and jeer at my son for not being 'cool'.

School uniform also explains why English girls dress so extravagantly at weekends. After dull maroon wool skirts all week no wonder they reach for the tacky silver T-shirt when it comes to the school disco. From one extreme to another.

Rewarding Mediocrity

The English show they are not very clever in the way they consistently praise the unpraiseworthy. I am talking of the high grades they randomly dish out for average achievement. So, the highest 'A' grade is awarded to one in five of all GCSE candidates, the English equivalent of our *'pas mal'* is 'very good', and *'insuffisant'* translates as 'well done!'.

In England 14/20 is a mediocre mark, while in France this is a very good grade. Our own stringent judging extends beyond education. Take the annual competition to find the best croissant in France. It was awarded two years running to the same *pâtisserie* in the 7th *arrondissement*. The judges' score? 14.5/20. However excellent, there was still room for improvement, which is how it should be. How will a child ever get on in the world if he is always patted on his back and told how wonderful he is?

The Absence of Failure

We are not afraid to use the word failure. An '*échec scolaire*', or scholastic failure is an accurate description of those who do not succeed at school. In England, there is no such thing, and failure is dressed up as special needs: dyslexia, dyspraxia. . .

'The Teacher Is Your Friend'

In France, we are clear. The teacher instructs and the children listen; there is discipline and structure. In England, they have the mistaken idea that there should be interaction, as though anyone should lay any store by what a young person thinks.

The Second World War Obsession

The French history curriculum is an examination of the key role played by France on the world's stage throughout the ages.

The English history curriculum covers just two periods: the Tudors, for younger children who like colouring in pictures of Henry VIII, and the Second World War for everyone else. I reject accusations that we French are sensitive about this period of our history. I always reply to any English person who dares to refer to 1940 that (a) you cannot know what it is like to be occupied, since you have the good fortune to be an island, and (b) just look how much more beautiful Paris is than London. Could the same be said if we had had the poor sense to let it be bombed?

The Second World War is exhaustively taught, and endlessly written about (just take a look at the wartime section in bookshops) because it was the last time the English ever felt good about themselves, and they don't want to forget it.

The Teenage Drinking Culture

Pierre-Edouard was invited to a sixteenth birthday party. When I dropped him off, I was amused to see the parents had hired 'bouncers' to manage the door, while they cowered upstairs in their bedroom. After hearing my son's shocked account of the evening, I understood why nightclub-style security was essential. Children passing out on the stairs, throwing bottles into the neighbours' gardens, vomiting on to the carpet: it was utterly *inadmissible*.

The party came to an end with the arrival of an ambulance crew to revive two young girls rendered senseless by vodka. Instead of being appalled, the paramedics were apparently most accommodating, discussing it with the parents as though it was a normal rite of passage. 'Well, we've all been there, haven't we?' one said, as she bundled them into the ambulance. Well, no we haven't, certainly not in France, where we would be ashamed to waste the *sapeurs pompiers'* time on dealing with the aftermath of our children's debauchery. Nor is this drunken behaviour limited to parties. One Englishwoman I know cannot leave her teenage son alone for an afternoon, in case he invites his mates round to empty the drinks cabinet. I blame the parents.

C'est très secret. . .Les rallyes!

When one sees bad behaviour condoned by English parents, one realizes action must be taken. Should we sit back and allow our children to fall in with this mindless binge-drinking culture? It would be taking cultural exchange one step too far!

So my friend Héloïse de pan de Rungis and I decided to organize *un rallye* to help our children meet the right sort: although we prefer not to use the term *rallye*, as it sounds snobbish and outdated. Quite simply, we drew up a list of boys and girls on a strictly non-selective basis, and asked their parents if they would be interested in joining *un cours de danse* (though we do advise discretion, as it might cause bitterness outside *les happy few*!).

I must say the results have been wonderful. The children learn bridge – so useful for getting on in *la bonne société* – and twice a week a *maître danseur* comes over on Eurostar to teach *le rock en ligne*. The parties are themed, for example 'chic choc!' when all the boys had to wear a brightly coloured shirt. Watching them twirl on the dance floor to the sounds of Eddy Mitchell gives me a great feeling of achievement. Here is *éducation* in the proper French sense.

Bee says, 'How old-fashioned and provincial, you're trying to turn your children into mini versions of yourself,' but I say, 'Better that than rolling around the streets drinking beer and throwing up.'

The Rise of the Baccalaureate

The English have seen sense at last and finally admitted that their 'A' level system, which enables children to give up maths at sixteen and still leave school with top grades, is far too limited. The baccalaureate is increasingly offered by private schools, but a word of warning here: it is *not* the French *baccalauréat*, but an easier one in English called the International Baccalaureate.

I remain unswerving in my belief in the French system: the sacrosanct three-part argument instilled at school that underpins all our rigorous thinking. The *baccalauréat français en option 'S'** remains the *voie royale* leading to success in every walk of life.

English Universities

The French education system is a triumph of meritocracy. Those with the highest grades rise to the top, like cream. And the *'crème de la crème'* (as the English call *le gratin*) win their places at *les grandes écoles* according to one pure criterion: how high they score in examinations. You do not have to be 'an interesting person'.

In England, where intellectual prowess is despised, they have the odd idea that the best university candidates are those who show evidence of being 'well rounded'. So parents pore over their children's 'personal statements', inventing hobbies and achievements to help them get ahead. It's rather like the Christmas 'round robin' letter, a one-off invitation to boast, before sinking back to their default mode of diffidence and self-deprecation.

---

*Translator's note: 'S' means the scientific option (the other two are Economics, 'ES', and Literature, or 'L'). All three options involve maths, but French families have been known to break down in crisis when a child has not chosen, or been selected for, the prestigious bac S.

One way English students seek to make themselves interesting is the 'gap year'. This *année sabbatique* apes the old aristocratic notion of the grand tour, but instead of admiring paintings in Rome and Madrid, teenagers make their parents pay for them to go and help out in a Third World school, or conservation project. Why that should make them a more valid candidate than a high maths grade, I do not know.

17

Mistrust of Intellectuals

'If they happen to rise above brag and whist, they
infallibly stop short of everything either pleasing or
instructive. I take the reason of this to be that our
English women are not nearly so well informed and
cultivated as the French.'

*Lord Chesterfield, praising the intellectual vigour of Parisian
salons in the 18th century*

The English are suspicious of intellectuals. Any
remark that rises slightly above the banal will
have you slapped down as a 'smart Alec', a 'clever
Dick' or 'too clever for your own good'. Crude bio-
logical language is used to remind the would-be
thinker that he is only a base animal, who is 'up his
own arse' or simply 'a wanker'.

Nothing gives the English more pleasure than
seeing a clever person failing to perform a simple
task: 'All those brains and not an ounce of common
sense!' For common sense is what the English pride
themselves on: dull, pragmatic, serviceable.

If you are French, and you try to lead the conversation out of the material and into the abstract, they'll jeer at you by making xenophobic references to your intellectual heritage.

'That's bit too Cartesian for me,' they'll say, or 'Spoken like an Existentialist!' Philosophy is rarely taught and widely feared.

'Intellectual' is Not a Job Title

'God is dead but my hair is perfect,' is the cruel jibe thrown at our own photogenic *intellectuel par excellence* Bernard-Henri Lévy. We may laugh at him, with his billowing open neck shirts, but at least he's there, along with the rest of France's modern thinkers (whose names momentarily escape me). We rightly look to our intellectuals to act as society's conscience and offer a non-partisan opinion.

In England, nobody calls himself or herself an intellectual. They might be a professor, a journalist, a historian, but they would never presume to claim intellectual status, as this would mean they were (a) boastful and (b) bad at their job, since being intellectual would impede them from what they should really be doing, which is climbing up the ladder of their particular profession. As Rousseau said, 'It is too difficult to think nobly when one thinks only of earning a living,' and earning a living is what the English think about most.

Bee says intellectuals are not welcomed by the British 'because we can't stand bores or pedants'. I didn't like the way she said it, nor the way she laughed and said it's been a long time since Camus when I failed to conjure up a list of living French intellectuals apart from BHL. Just go into the right Parisian cafés, I said, and you'll see them. To which Bee replied that she always found the Left Bank cafés full of morose silent people, and the occasional irritable outburst and finger-wagging was not to be confused with mind-expanding conversation. Really, she can be most irritating.

Dinner-Party Conversation

In my early days in London, we were invited to dinner by a BBC producer and her barrister husband. The other guests included a distinguished professor and a prize-winning author. How wonderful, I said to Pierre-Marie, that we will be mixing with the English intelligentsia, at last we can expect some stimulating conversation. How naïve I was!

Dinner-party conversation is best summarized as trivial chit-chat. It starts with the guests' journeys.

We might ask how long it took them to get there, which transport method was favoured. Then we might broaden out, still strictly on the personal, 'How was your day?' This will be a cue for an amusing anecdote from the office, preferably delivered with a black note of despair, and a healthy dose of self-deprecation. Silly old me, is the message, I'm just so stupid. Fancy leaving the papers on his desk where everyone could read them! Being French, I will think *quel con,* you *are* a damn fool for leaving the papers in the wrong place, but everyone else will rush in with approval and sympathy, 'Oh dear, how awful,' etc. Then we'll talk about how much the house next door has just sold for.

Fear of being a bore keeps the talk swift and quick-changing, and by necessity superficial. After laughter at the government's latest blunder, culture may be touched upon, as in 'Have you seen the new play at the National?', to which the reply may be 'No, I hear it's really good', or 'Yes, it was really up itself.' But there is no in-depth analysis. Is it because they are ignorant (bear in mind these people were all graduates of top universities) or is it because it is bad manners to 'show off' by expressing an informed opinion?

At just one moment the conversation took a slightly higher turn, when finally two people engaged in a discussion about whether it was morally appropriate for an artist to use the body parts of consenting deceased adults; but alas, I cut it short. Having drunk one more glass of wine that I would normally (often the case here), I made the mistake of saying how pleased we were to find ourselves dining with the London intelligentsia. Roars of laughter ensued, and talk swiftly moved back to how much X earned, who said what to whom, and whether little Molly was likely to get into her first choice of school.

Now, I don't want to appear too partisan, but is it not the case that the French dinner table is a forum for passionately exchanged opinions on a wide range of subjects? A place where the pedestrian is rejected in favour of higher debate? The nearest you'll find in England is the *café philo* they occasionally hold in the French Institute. And that's another idea the Brits find side-splittingly funny: an open discussion about philosophical matters? You're joking, aren't you?

A Tale of Two Press Conferences

There were two press conferences in the same English hotel: one for Nelson Mandela, world icon for human rights, the other for Jade Goody, runner-up in the TV show *Big Brother*. Guess which one was full to bursting?

French Celebrities vs English Celebrities

It is instructive to compare a list of English and French celebrities, and to see which qualities are required to succeed in the two cultures.

FRENCH CELEBRITIES (MOSTLY DEAD, BUT STILL REVERED)

Serge Gainsbourg: musician, intellectual and heavy smoker, described by Mitterand as 'our Apollinaire'

Jean-Paul Sartre: philosopher, world famous intellectual and heavy smoker

Bernard-Henri Lévy: philosopher, intellectual and ex-heavy smoker

Catherine Deneuve: beautiful actress, brainy icon, ex-heavy smoker

Gérard Depardieu; real man actor, *côté primaire* intellectual, winemaker and heavy smoker

Michel Houellebecq: writer, intellectual and heavy smoker

Camus: best writer ever, incarnation of the intellectual, heavy smoker

Jean-Luc Godard: cinéaste, intellectual god and heavy smoker

Bernard Kouchner: human rights medical person, now engaged by Sarkozy's government

Napoleon: the greatest general ever, but also fiercely intellectual, whose Code is still the basis of our great republic

We need not count Johnny Halliday, as he is Belgian, and also he left France to become a tax exile in Switzerland.

ENGLISH CELEBRITIES

Jade Goody: *Big Brother* contestant, an ordinary girl taken to the hearts of the English by virtue of her staggering ignorance, now a TV star 'in her own right'

David Beckham: loved for being witless, having a celebrity wife, and playing football

Liz Hurley: loved for wearing that dress and for once being the girlfriend of silly ass actor Hugh Grant

Kate Moss: model, loved for behaving like a teenage binge drinker.

18

Mistrust of Culture

'Culture: the cry of men in face of
their destiny.'
Albert Camus

The English grow weary at the mention of 'culture'. Talk knowledgeably about the arts and you'll be branded 'a Culture Vulture', an ugly old bird digging over a corpse that should be left alone. 'Culture' is a worthy bolt-on to a beach holiday, a hard seat in a theatre, a medicine you have to take.

Whereas in France, we live and breathe culture. It's the same word, but sounds so much better in French, '*culture*', rolling off the tongue in a loving murmur, instead of the guttural, choking 'Kull-tcher'.

Minister for Culture. . . and Sport and Media and Tourism

When André Malraux became our first *Ministre de Culture* in 1960, he declared 'I am France' and opened *centres culturels* he described as 'the cathedrals of the twentieth century'. Jack Lang continued the evangelical passion in 1981, rejoicing that 'The French have crossed the frontier separating darkness from light.'

The English didn't get a Ministry of Culture until 1997* and even then they lumped it in with sport, tourism and media, and no prizes for guessing which bits they prefer. Casinos, football, and lurid newspaper headlines: here is what passes for culture in this barbaric society.

English culture can be divided into two: high, which everyone pretends to like, but finds very boring, and low, which everyone enjoys, though smug types will pretend they are enjoying in an 'ironic' way.

High Culture

High culture in England means two things. Shakespeare and Opera.

SHAKESPEARE

'A powerful, fruitful genius . . .without a spark of good
taste or least knowledge of the rules.' *Voltaire, describing
Shakespeare in his Lettres philosophiques.*

*Until then it was known as the Department of National Heritage – looking back at musty old houses – which is what the English like.

Shakespeare is always cited by English people as proof of their love of culture. From the Royal Shakespeare Company to school plays to local amateur productions, there he is, endlessly recycled.

Coyly known as The Bard, he is used as a stick with which to beat the French: the richness of his vocabulary! The unfettered power of his imagination! His anarchic mix of tragedy and comedy! Better than Racine, eh?

To compare Shakespeare with Racine is like asking us to choose between a big messy mongrel and a pedigree poodle: an untamed wilderness or the tightly controlled *parc* of Versailles. As André Gide put it, 'Racine inspires me with an emotion that Sakespeare never gives me – the emotion that comes from perfection.'

So is he any good? To paraphrase Voltaire (who introduced him to the French, but later dismissed him as 'the drunken savage') there are pearls in the *ordures*, but a great deal of *ordures*. Shakespeare didn't bother about the classic unities: unlike Racine, who wrote for the court, he wrote to entertain the brawling 'groundlings' who rolled in from the pub – and it shows. Vulgar language, crude jokes, and shameless crowd-pleasing detract from the undeniable vigour of the poetry. We had the right idea in eighteenth-century France when we added ballet to *King Lear*, to make it more refined.

Here are the facets of Shakespeare that continue to make him so popular with the English:

• Cross-dressing: men getting an erotic charge from women dressed as boys

• Violent thuggery: ugly scenes of butchery and hammy sword fights onstage, unheard of in French classical drama where all action is filtered from afar.

• Drunks on stage: inebriated grave-diggers, lowlife characters laughing and swearing. These indecorous scenes were removed from early French productions of Shakespeare.

• Bad jokes: it may have been funny four hundred years ago, but lumbering around the stage in a pair of yellow stockings no longer cuts it. Unless you're English of course.

• Domestic detail: dropped hankies, mice and rats, references to jelly and greasy pots: the English passion for sitcom is well satisfied. They're far happier with this kind of trivia than highbrow abstract ideas.

In summary, I would advise you not to bother with the comedies – Molière has far more *esprit* and fewer plodding misunderstandings. The tragedies are a different matter, and I must agree with Victor Hugo (who wanted Shakespeare to be crowned poet laureate of the united states of Europe) that here we see the founder of modernism, 'the torrent that has burst its banks', breaking down the barriers of classical drama.

My favourite Shakespeare play is *Hamlet*, because there is something almost French in the sensibility of this archetypical modern hero ('sulky' is how Bee puts it). However, the play is far too long, with unnecessary details that a more rigorous dramatist would have removed. Racine would have made a better job of it.

There have been a number of unfortunate by-products of Shakespeare:

• Thespian 'loveyness': English actors are very affected, and pretend to be superstitious about *Macbeth*, referring to it as 'the Scottish Play'. They also use abbreviations : '*The Dream*', '*The Shrew*'. . .

• Shakespeare heritage sights: the Globe Theatre – a piece of Disney-esque kitsch, built on the river, *en plein milieu* of London (at least we built Disneyland at a decent distance from Paris in the middle of a flat farmland desert).

• Stratford upon Avon – Shakespeare's birthplace and now home to a million tour buses. *A éviter.*

GLYNDEBOURNE: L'OPÉRA PIQUE-NIQUE

The English don't care for high culture, and love to disguise it as something else.

Take opera. Potentially long and boring, it also poses the problem of whether one should eat before or after the performance. The pragmatic English have found the perfect solution: pretend it's a garden party, and break it up with a two-hour picnic in the grounds of a country mansion. And just to make it more eccentric, you have to wear full evening dress.

Pierre-Marie and I have been entirely seduced by this *très British* institution and our 'season' always includes a visit to Glyndebourne. Last year, we took the train, where we engaged with two City traders and their blonde companions who were becoming what they termed as 'suitably refreshed' with the aid of two magnums of Veuve Clicquot from their hamper which they graciously shared with us. One was wearing tartan trousers he claimed 'had shrunk in the wash', which I took as a humorous allusion to his bulging waistline. As the bottles went down, so their conversation became more animated, with talk of their estates in Scotland, buying property in Berlin, and whether they should attend Annabel's or Bouji's nightclub later on. There was no talk of opera. One of them took out a camera and aimed it at the blondes (east European, twenty years his junior).

'Say sex, girls,' he said, 'there, that made them smile.' He then pulled out some photos to show them his private jet.

Pierre-Marie confirmed when we left the train that they were indeed examples of the overpaid City workers who gave his profession a bad name. I thought they were rather fun.

THE PICNIC

A trip to Glyndebourne has nothing to do with the opera, and everything to do with the picnic. The English have always adored picnics because it is cheaper than eating in a restaurant, fits in with their self-denying philosophy of 'making do', and forces them to cope with adversity (weather, discomfort, etc).

Here are the rules for the picnic. Bear in mind the inconvenience is maximized by the silk dresses and tuxedos that are the least suitable clothes for the occasion.

1. Park the car as far as possible from the picnic site. This means you must struggle across the grass with your hamper, chairs, cool box, rugs, plastic sheets, table, spangly gold handbag, etc. At Glyndebourne much snobbery is attached to where you install your picnic: near the car is frowned

upon, round the lake is preferable, entailing a fifteen-minute hike.

2. Whatever you do, don't go for the rain-proof tables in the tent. This is considered cheating.

3. Organize English weather. This means the grass will be muddy and you are likely to slip over in the rain and ruin your outfit and squash the picnic at the same time.

4. Wear high-heeled strappy sandals, and a thin dress so you shiver on the groundsheet. If there is a heat-wave, at least your husband will suffer, as etiquette will not allow him to remove his dinner jacket.

5. On no account order the in-house service, where waiters set up a table for you at the edge of the haha and bring you lobster, champagne etc. This is far too civilized – dare I say, *French* – and not at all in the Dunkirk spirit.

6. Enjoy looking at what people are wearing. It's an insight into the English class system. Old money wears floral prints and battered old DJs and eats frugal Marks & Spencer sandwiches. New money arrives late with its corporate clients, misses the first act and passes with relief directly to its flashy picnic prepared by Harvey Nicks. It wears glossy

designerwear. The best dressed people are French, as always.

7. Don't bring your chauffeur. This means that one grumpy member of your party will be unable to drink, and will face a two-hour drive back to London.

Low Culture

TELEVISION

Let me admit right away that I absolutely adore English television. Very often, Pierre-Marie and I prepare ourselves a 'TV supper' and sit down for a quiet night in, to wonder at the humiliation that people will put themselves through to get on 'telly'. 'Ordinary people' (but aren't all people ordinary?) throw themselves into the ring, to be built up, then smashed down by the cruel gods of public opinion. It is an opportunity to wallow in the national shame, and feel just a little bit superior.

We had *Big Brother* once on French television. We called it *Loft Story* and found it moderately diverting as a social experiment. We did not see the need to repeat it nine times over! We prefer to engage with our own lives, not voyeuristically look at other people's.

BOOKS

Books listed under 'low culture'? It wouldn't happen in France, but then we like to read about ideas, not the abused childhood of a dysfunctional TV celebrity.

I love to call in at the French bookshops in South Kensington to pick up a Gallimard novel, so severe in its plain, pale orange cover, adorned only by a Goncourt winner's red belly band. Or a slim *essai*, a hundred pages devoted to one single, cogently argued thesis.

I enjoy making cultural comparisons, for instance between the philosophical reflexions of *La vie sexuelle de Catherine M.* and the smutty call girl tales of *Belle de Jour*[†]. Many English books are decorated with silly cartoons, to appeal to those who fear a book may prove 'too heavy'.

Only 3 percent of books published in England are translated from other languages, compared with 25 percent in France. Bee said this must be because France hasn't got enough writers of its own, which is completely missing the point. We have *l'esprit ouvert*: our minds are opened to the world. Whereas the English remain bogged down in the parochial smallness of their TV screens.

[†]As usual, the English use a French title to denote sexual material.

FILMS

As a Frenchwoman in London, I have been subjected to all kinds of xenophobic attacks, on a very personal level. As though it were I, Hortense de Monplaisir, who had personally resumed nuclear tests in the Pacific, burned vanloads of British sheep and signed the 1940 treaty!

Of all the many slurs upon our culture, the one I am most tired of hearing is the jealous tirade against our wonderful film industry. Here are some typical complaints:

1. *Your* French films (as though I had directed every one of them) are incomprehensible and boring, all about depressed Parisians sitting on the edges of beds and saying nothing.

2. Anyone can make a film in France, the government hands out grants for any old rubbish.

To which I reply as follows: Guy Ritchie and Richard Curtis. Mindless gun culture and stammering sexual inadequacy.

The only good English films are made for children (of all ages), like the *Carry On* films, *Mary Poppins* and *The Sound of Music*. Which brings me to another extraordinary English night out:

SINGALONGA SOUNDA MUSIC

The English are children at heart, and enjoy getting together for a good singsong, even in terrible circumstances. Our own troops were astonished in the First World War, to see English troops singing in the trenches, finding humour in adversity as they made up silly names for foreign towns they couldn't pronounce (Ypres became 'Wipers'). You find them these days on the football terrace, where young men invent playground-style songs to taunt the opposition, and participatory singing is often favoured above a professional *chorale*. Bee tells me that when she was a child, her favourite TV show was a recreation of the Victorian Music Hall, a *comédie musicale* where the audience dressed up in crinolines and bonnets to indulge themselves in group renditions of 'Daisy, Daisy', and 'Roll out the Barrel'*.

It was in a bid to recapture this spirit that Bee persuaded us to accompany her and her husband to an extraordinary evening in Leicester Square. We were advised to dress up as characters from the film *The Sound of Music*, so I hired a décolleté *mädchen* style outfit with a thick black belt that emphasized

---

*Old Cockney songs that the English cannot resist. reinforcing their idealized view of the traditional working class as a 'chirpy chappy', poor but happy.

my small waist, while Pierre-Marie cut a dash in an Austrian admiral's uniform that looked perfect beneath the green woollen Loden coat that he always wears to the office. Bee wore a nun's habit and Hereward squeezed himself into a tight pair of *lederhosen*.

The moment we arrived at the cinema, we realized that we were conspicuously over-dressed. Far from being the *bal masqué* that we envisaged, this was clearly little more than another drunken night out for a clientele of young English people, nearly all of them in their usual clothes. Even now, I blush to remember Pierre-Marie's facial muscles tensing as he sensed that this was not going to be his kind of evening. He cannot bear to feel ridiculous, and as he was handed his bag of 'props' (sprig of cardboard edelweiss, scrap of material representing the curtains used by Maria to make dresses for the von Trapp children) I squeezed his hand and whispered in his ear that never again would I put him through such an ordeal.

I have kept true to that promise (I excused him the visit to the pantomime, for instance) and as the drag artist performed the warm-up routine, encouraging us to give full voice to Doh-a-deer, as though we were still in the *maternelle*, I realized the enormous gulf that separated us from our English neighbours. We behave like adults, whereas they love any excuse to revert to *l'infantilisme*, singing their hearts out, wallowing in childhood memories, and wishing life could be as simple as it was when they first saw Julie Andrews smiling like a saint in that appalling haircut.

19

The Nostalgia Disease

'Things aren't what they were.'
Universal moan on the streets
of England

France is a modern country*. We move bravely on, embracing daring new architecture and radical reduced working hours, whilst preserving our great traditions: food, monuments, the right of man to go on demonstrations. Although naturally, it all stops for dinner. I was recently trapped in Le Bon Marché during a *manifestation* but was released at *l'heure de l'apéritif*, which goes to show how considerate the French are in their pursuit of democracy.

*My neighbour Bee argues that France is not modern at all, but stuck in the past. She says that's why English people buy houses there, because it's quaint and reminds them of how England used to be, but that shows how little she knows. We have just kept hold of what is worth having, which is not the same as freezing the past in aspic.

England, on the other hand, appears to be modern, with its funky cosmopolitanism and childlike enthusiasm for anything new (don't talk to this Frenchwoman about their defection to New World wines!), but remains emotionally enslaved to the past. Here is how:

The Royal Family

What possible purpose for keeping them except as a sentimental reminder of past glories? And I *categorically* refute those silly accusations that we envy the British and wish we had our own monarchy back. We already tried that and it didn't work. Though it goes without saying that if we did still have a royal family, it would be more elegant than the house of Windsor.

While not personally acquainted with the royals, I was once invited to a private shopping evening at the Prince of Wales's residence Clarence House. (My republican principles were briefly put aside as I wanted some limited edition teacups for Pierre-Marie's parents, who are rather *ancien régime* in their sympathies, even though they cannot lay claim to a noble lineage like mine.)

I was ushered through a police check, past the empty, dark rooms of this magnificent palace, and was welcomed by a group of lady volunteers, up from the country to run the Christmas sale. Were they sleeping at the palace, I asked? – there being plenty of space after all and nobody at home. No, no, they said, it wouldn't be appropriate, they'd stay in a hotel (and thereby no doubt eat into the charity proceeds of the sale). Did I feel, off with the royal heads? I did.

The English respect for royalty is deeply engrained. Watch the performers at the Royal Variety Show queuing up to cringe in gratitude as they are presented to a royal; see the crowds lay out their sleeping bags on the pavement to ensure a good view of a royal wedding. Observe the unctuous manner of the royal servants, the expression that says 'I'm better than you because I get to hold the royal toothbrush.' It flies in the face of everything we have stood for since 1789 and points out that the English are a bunch of retro-toadies, in love with the pageantry of the past. *Vive la revolution!*

However, I did buy some exquisite plants from the Highgrove Garden, and my tea service was graciously received. Oh, and Prince Charles appeared really quite *raffiné* in the flesh when I actually caught a glimpse of him at the opera, and we must admit there is an almost French sensibility in the aesthetic presentation of some of his Duchy of Cornwall range of food products.

The National Trust

For a truly English day out, you must take a Sunday afternoon visit to an historic stately home. You will join carloads of nostalgia addicts whose favourite weekend activity is coming to gawp at the wonderful houses their betters used to inhabit.

Manor houses, castles, even humble writers' cottages, all are restored with the inimitable English gift for wallowing in the past. Each room is guarded by a volunteer, who behaves like a *châtelaine*, pacing around grandly and offering snippets of information about what she considers her spiritual home, if only she had been born in an earlier, fairer age.

Once you have shuffled through the upstairs rooms, you head down to the kitchens where copper pans and model dead rabbits remind you that you could have been happy here, too, even a servant's lot being preferable to the bleakness of your modern bungalow. Then you go for a slap-up tea of scones with clotted cream, served up in the stables by Victorian wenches.

Finally, the Shop gives you the opportunity to buy a little piece of whimsy and take it home: a 'mouse-to-mouse resuscitation' tea towel (with an amusing picture of a mouse pouring a glass of wine down another's throat), a tapestry teacosy with matching tankard jug 'containing a full imperial pint' (as opposed to a deceitful continental half-litre), crocheted bowl covers, pot pourri, Beatrix Potter placemats, coasters made from old 78 records, even a game called Reminiscing. All designed to sustain the feel-good nostalgic glow of a visit to a stately home.

Nearly all of these houses belong to the UK's biggest private landowner, the National Trust. As sleek and fat as any *ancien régime* aristocrat, this charity is hugely rich, with three-and-a-half million paid-up members, twelve million annual visitors to its pay-to-visit properties and a generous income from legacies.

While French *châteaux* – mostly seized during the revolution – are run by functionaries along municipal no-nonsense lines, National Trust houses still have the feel of family houses, where you should speak in a hushed voice and brush the mud off your shoes before going in for an audience with his Lordship. It's as if England's entire heritage has been bought up by a benevolent gentleman, who will allow visitors, provided they behave themselves.

No commercial outlet is left untapped. You can rent a National Trust cottage, send NT Christmas cards, and even decorate your home with National Trust paint in the very colours favoured by bygone lords and ladies. *Noblesse oblige!*

The TV Costume Drama

The English love costume dramas, and their favourite pin-up actors are those who look good in bodices and breeches. The past, it seems, was so much sexier. Colin Firth, Helena Bonham Carter, Hugh Grant, Keira Knightley, Emma Thompson, Catherine Zeta-Jones, Jeremy Irons all consolidated their careers by looking handsome in a great big old house.

Opposition to Road-building

In France, we are proud to celebrate the opening of a new motorway, and no one cheers more loudly than the local people it serves. The English take a different view. They whine and moan and would have us living back in the age of the horse and cart. Why can't it be like the good old days, they complain, when the only way to get to London involved five horse relays at coaching inns?

Of course, this is deeply hypocritical. They love their cars, they love the freedom to drive around the country, but they wish the road wasn't *quite* so close to their precious back garden. These objectors are called nimbys (Not In My Back Yard) by English people living at a safer distance from the proposed new road.

Romanticizing the Working Class

'We were poor but happy,' is what the English like to believe when looking back over the wretched life of the common man. The servants' annual outing to the seaside, the Cockneys' hop-picking 'holidays' in Kent, the convivial ale house: all celebrated as care-free occasions, where everyone 'rolled out the barrel', 'packed their troubles in their old kit bag' and had a 'good old singsong'.

If we are sometimes accused of *morosité* in our attitude and our artistic output, it can only be that we refuse to go along with this reactionary myth.

Second World War

Again! Please, can you just move on and think about something else!

Mais Quand Même:

There are also good things to be found in their attachment to the past.

The atmosphere of the stately home also reminds us of the grandeur that was France, and we must admit that the English are good at the past.

Fleur de Lys candles and notepaper from the National Trust shop/catalogue are always acceptable.

The English are less insistent on those tape-recorded guides clamped to every visitor's ears in French *chateâux*.

To wallow in the spectacle of an English costume drama can make a refreshing change from our own tense tales of modern existential angst.

20

Pets, Their One True Love

A man's best friend
is his dog.
English proverb

An enduring image for us is the Englishman with his dog, a solitary figure walking around his country estate, at peace with the world and mercifully freed from the need to make conversation.

In town he cuts a more emasculated figure: stooping into the gutter, 'poop scoop' in hand, behind his squatting pet. In Paris, we have dashing green suited men on motorbikes to vacuum up the dog mess; in London they have little municipal dustbins where obedient citizens dispose of their 'dogs' doings'.

The toughest Englishman melts at the sight of an animal. I was having tea at a friend's house while her wall was being repaired by a tattooed builder of gargantuan proportions. She took him out a cup of tea, the way they always do, and found him tenderly stroking her kitten.

'They're lovely, aren't they?' he murmured, helping himself to a rich tea biscuit.

Where we use the term *animal domestique*, the English have adopted the noun 'pet', from the verb to 'pet', which means to stroke, kiss and cuddle. Make no doubt about it, these animals are objects of their most powerful feelings.

In France we have dogs for one of two reasons. Either it is a big brute, chained to a kennel to guard our property, barking constantly to reinforce the menacing message of the *chien méchant* sign affixed to our gate. Or it is a fluffy accessory chosen to enhance our glamour when we step out on to the streets of Paris. In neither case do we treat the animal as a human being, with 'rights'.

The 'rights' of English dogs include being taken for very long walks, whereas we are perfectly happy to keep them in the apartment all day, with just a brief outing for *ses besoins*. Can you believe there are people here who earn a living as 'dog-walkers'?

It is harder for a school leaver to be accepted on a veterinary training course than it is to get into medical school. The English vet offers his patients five-star luxury treatment far removed from the NHS. Assisted by his nurses, he treats the animal like an emotionally fragile child, with the kind of soft words and nurturing that would be considered 'making a fuss' if it were directed at a human being. He must never pick up a cat by the scruff of his neck, and full anaesthesia is standard for the most minor procedure. It is routine to neuter dogs and cats, ostensibly to 'keep them safe', though I put it down to the general English distaste for sex. Certainly, there is something limp – and very un-French – about the way English dogs never attack each other in parks.

Not only do English animals receive superior health care, they also eat better than their owners, thanks to the rise of gourmet pet food. Just look at the contents of a pensioner's supermarket basket: Oh So Tasty duck in gravy for pussy, and an indifferent frozen pie for madam.

Sentimentality about animals also makes the English squeamish about their own diet. There are many so-called vegetarians who 'only eat chicken', presumably because cows, lambs and pigs remind them too much of their pets. They are particularly dewy-eyed about veal, which is rarely available. And whereas we keep the same vocabulary for animals and meat, they adopt a French derivative noun to define the culinary version of an Anglo-Saxon beast: so a cow becomes beef, a pig becomes pork, a sheep becomes mutton. And you should see their eyes widen in horror at the sight of a horsemeat butcher! Regrettably, English settlers in France are also importing their sentimental ideas about animals, opening donkey sanctuaries, lost cat homes, etc.

News programmes often end with a heart-warming tale involving a pet animal. The same journalist who has just savaged a politican will smile indulgently as he announces the news that a kitten has been rescued from a rooftop. Every year people die diving into the sea to rescue a dog which has slipped off a cliff path. Her Majesty the Queen leads the way, coldly shaking hands with her six-year-old son, but shedding tears for a dead stag*. When one of her corgis was fatally injured by her daughter's dog it was headline news for a week. From the Monarch downwards, they really do prefer animals to people.

*As fictionalized in Stephen Frears' film *The Queen*.

21

The English on Holiday

'The great and recurrent question about abroad is,
is it worth getting there?'

Rose Macaulay

For us, the choice of where to go on holiday is very simple. We ask ourselves one question: *mer, montagne ou campagne?* Sea, mountain or country-side. All in France, naturally: there is no need to go further, though we may take some winter sun in the French West Indies where the food is reliable. Other destinations are decided for us by Club Med, who have made *L'Etranger* more palatable by installing *la culture française* in identikit resorts around the world.

The English know no such restrictions. Sometimes I envy them the giddy excitement with which they seek out the latest 'hot' destination to invade with their guidebook and bulging suitcase. The world is truly their oyster. They have no obligation to return to the same beach on Ile de Ré because that's where the family always goes, and it won't be the same if the fifteen cousins don't all sit down to lunch together every day.

The English Seaside Holiday

To understand the English enthusiasm for foreign holidays, take a look at what they had to put up with before the advent of cheap air travel. Advertisements for windswept coastal resorts used to make a virtue of their miserable climate: 'Come to Great Yarmouth, it's *so* bracing!'

Let me explain to you the significance of the 'windbreak'. This essential piece of beach equipment is a canvas screen that the English erect on their home beaches to keep out the howling wind. Shivering in their swimsuits, they huddle behind it, nursing a Thermos of hot tea, and trying to pretend they are having fun, in spite of overwhelming evidence that the British climate* is entirely unsuited to beach holidays.

In order to keep warm they eat constantly, and if you think their regular diet is eccentric, you should

---

*Translators' Note. Our recent hot summers here have failed to alter Hortense's perception of England as a cold place. We must allow her poetic licence.

see how it evolves on holiday. I was once invited to stay in Cornwall, and here is what I ate:

• Breakfast (the only meal you eat at the table): fruit juice, cereal, bacon, egg, sausage, potato cake, fried bread, toast and marmalade.

• Lunch: Cornish pasty (a huge meat and potato pastry designed as fuel-food for miners to eat at the coal-face, but now eaten in the car, staring out at the rain), followed by a bar of chocolate-style confectionery.

• Tea: a dangerous threat to the arteries: 'scones' stuffed with clotted cream and jam.

• Dinner: fish and chips.

When I returned, I had to take an emergency trip to my favourite spa in La Baule for a *cure de thalassothérapie* to repair the damage.

Concerned about their carbon footprints (see my chapter on puritans), many English are now choosing to take their holidays at home. Just for fun, Pierre-Marie and I thought we should do the same, and spent a most successful mini-break at Babington House hotel in Devon, so chic it could almost have been designed by our own Jacques Garcia. The other guests were both modern and *raffinés*, I really could not fault it.

Encouraged by this venture, we booked a weekend in Brighton: a Bohemian coastal town, popular with artists and actors. We imagined it might be the equivalent of Trouville. My dears, what a contrast! If you want an accurate snapshot of England at leisure, I urge you to take a walk down the pier. A pier, in case you are not familiar with the term, is a long *jetée* filled with the most gross entertainments you can imagine. Slot machine arcades, fish and chips, a disco, seedy deckchairs where you sink down with your cans of beer and sausage rolls. Utterly engrossing. We returned on the train to London, which looked the very acme of civilization by comparison. That was three years ago and we have not left the city since, except to return to France.

English Sunseekers Abroad

Old habits die hard, and the English bring the same 'survival' tactics to their new foreign destinations, forgetting that what works on the windswept shores of Wales is inappropriate when it's 34 degrees in the shade.

Determined to make things as difficult as possible, they heave bags of food, newspapers, beach games, buckets and spades and pushchair across the scorching sands to set up camp at the furthest point. While the French are packing up for lunch, the English will be spreading sunblock over their fair skins and stretching out in the searing heat, before running, shrieking into the sea. By four o'clock, they will be scorched scarlet, in spite of the sunblock, and retreating in search of shade and *pommes frites* because their snack lunch has left them needing 'something to keep them going' until dinner.

How very different from our own sensible approach. Naturally, we park just two minutes' walk from the beach umbrella that we have rented *pour la saison*. And naturally we will spend the hottest part of the day in a restaurant, allowing time for *la bonne digestion* before we return to take our afternoon swim at the optimum time, for avoiding sun damage to our perfectly tanned skins.

Germanophobia

One thing I adore about the English is their respect for our good taste. It is flattering to be told that they take their holidays in France or 'places where French people go', because they know the food will be good and the behaviour civilized. What greater tribute can there be to our elegance and *savoir faire*? And how wonderful that we are still considered a shining example of how things should be done, setting the standard across the globe.

In sharp contrast is their marked prejudice against the Germans. As far as I can tell, this is for one reason. It is because – so they claim – the Germans go down to the pool before breakfast to monopolize all the sunloungers by spreading their towels over them. I cannot tell you how often I have heard this complaint; it seems to have the entire country simmering in collective resentment! Whether or not it is true, I could not say. But I do know that if I want to lie on a sunlounger and there is a towel already on it, I do the obvious thing. I remove the towel and replace it with my own. (If only the English could shake off their old-fashioned respect for the 'first come, first served' rule, they could lose their distaste for staying in hotels alongside our European neighbours!)

The English also accuse the Germans of gathering outside the dining room so as to be first into dinner, then overdoing it at the all-you-can-eat buffet. I have to say this is classic case of 'the pot calling the kettle black'*. Personally, I would rather risk staying in a hotel with German sunseekers than English. Though I love them dearly as individuals, the English *en*

*English expression for blaming others who have the same fault.

masse, on holiday in a country where the drink is cheap, are a terrifying prospect, which is why Spain has become a no-go area for all French people.

Holiday Bulimics

Budget flights have given rise to another English addication: the mini-break*. Why would you not fly to Perpignan for the weekend when it only costs £15? You'd spend that on tube fares in London.

As a result, England has become a place where everyone is constantly arranging to be somewhere else. On the internet, on their mobile phones, booking flights, hotels. The country has turned into a giant airport.

The desire for the mini-break soon becomes an obligation. I'm so exhausted, the English say, I need a Break. Then they exhaust themselves researching where to go for the Break, getting the best deal, putting in the hours to earn the Break. And believe me, Stansted airport at five in the morning is not where you want to be. A giant queue snaking round endless barriers ensures that many people miss their flights, which will not be refunded. And then they

*Mini-break does not translate into French, we only have *les vacances*.

have to run on to the plane to secure their seats and *buy* undrinkable coffee and rubber sandwiches from a hostess who would not be employed to clean the floors of Air France.

So much for the glamour of travel.

Once Again, the French Have Got it Right!

Would it be too self-congratulatory to remind ourselves of the way our year pans out, with its perfect rhythm?

To recap briefly: all serious work is achieved between *la rentrée* in September and the February skiing holiday. After this, we wait for *les beaux jours* to return in May, when we have four public holidays, so everyone can profit from long weekends in the country. June is a month of warm nights on Paris terraces, and blissful anticipation of July and August, when the entire country goes off for the *grandes vacances*.

No room for a mini-break there!

22

Christmas

'Christmas is a holiday that persecutes the lonely, the frayed and the rejected.'

Jimmy Cannon

We French have always had a talent for feeling the rhythm of the year, taking the pleasures of each season, in a correct and refined away.

Let us consider the discreet family celebration that is Christmas as we know it in France. We assemble on the evening of 24th December, around an elegant menu based on *la mer* or *la terre* – oysters and seafood, or perhaps *foie gras* and game. A convivial atmosphere, a few presents exchanged. The next morning, we may go to church. And the day after that, we go back to work.

Now let me talk you through Christmas, English style. All the pleasure that we spread into daily life over the year, they condense into one enormous over-the-top binge.

It begins in September when restaurants start taking bookings for office Christmas lunches and catalogues fall through your letterbox reminding you there are only 81 shopping days to go. By October, the shop windows are bulging with stockings saying 'I've been very very good', and private in-store shopping evenings in November invite you to 'get ahead' and 'beat the crowds' before the great rush. You are urged to 'get in the Christmas spirit' by buying whisky (a *jeu de mots** on *l'esprit* and alcohol). Cookery magazines offer inadequate British cooks hints on the 'countdown to Christmas' to help them get a turkey into the oven.

It is a ghastly exercise in panic and materialistic fervour, so debilitating that no one can go to work for ten days afterwards. And yet there is 'no peace for the wicked', as they remind themselves in jocular submission to the next stage of the festivities. Two days after Christmas, they are at it again, as they take off for the sales. Customers queue patiently in Marks & Spencer to return their Christmas presents in order to buy them again at half price, and stand patiently on cold pavements to be first in to snap up the 'bargains', including half-price crackers for next year's celebrations.

---

*Translator's note: pun. The French were very keen on puns in the Versailles era, but there is less scope for them now, with their rationalized, reduced vocabulary.

Here are some particular aspects of Christmas in England that explain why I invariably return to France for *les fêtes*.

Christmas Cards

A ritual designed to give offence. The English keep lists of who they send cards to, and get offended if they are not reciprocated. They also suffer guilt pangs if they receive cards from people not on their list.

A new variation on the Christmas card is the round robin letter, in which women boast about their family's achievements. This is quite contrary to the usual English practice of false modesty. The Christmas spirit allows them to discard conventional manners and brag about their holidays, their husband's promotion and their children's sporting achievements.

The Office Christmas Party

Poor Pierre-Marie, I will never forget him coming home from his first office Christmas party in London. In Paris, it was not unknown for him to have a swift *petit apéritif* with his colleagues before the holidays, but nothing prepared him for this. At five o'clock, all the women in the office disappeared into the lavatories and emerged dressed like call girls in glittery low-cut dresses, decorated with garlands of tinsel or novelty Santa motifs. Once at the venue, everyone set about getting 'bladdered'. Naturally awkward, the English relied on alcohol to enable conversation and it was accepted that the only way to get through the evening was to become 'rat-arsed'. Pot luck gifts were allocated and Pierre-Marie received a furry 'willy warmer*' in the guise of a reindeer. The dancing, he said, was unfathomable, with the women lurching around together, falling out of their dresses and men pretending to play the electric guitar. He tried to bring some elegance to the proceedings by inviting several girls to partner him in *le rock*, but not one of them knew how to dance properly and laughed at him for being old fashioned!

Unable to find a cab, he took the tube home, picking his way through groups of girls falling off their high heels, and inebriates dribbling on to their office suits. The ultimate degradation of the evening, he said, was when the tube stopped at Piccadilly Circus, the doors opened just long enough for a man in a Father Christmas hat to vomit into the carriage,

*A kind of novelty condom fashioned from fake fur, in compliance with the English belief that *les genitaux* are a subject for ridicule.

before the doors closed and the train moved on. *Quelle vulgarité!*

Over-indulgence

One lesson the English refuse to learn from us is the importance of restraint. The obligatory 'Christmas blow out' will see them staggering, groaning, from the table after a roast dinner with an unnecessary number of rich accompaniments, followed by a pudding of a heaviness unknown in French cuisine. The same intemperance is shown in drink, and in expense on lavish gifts.

This bulimic frenzy is followed by self-flagellation in January. Diets and hangover cures are advertised, credit card bills pile up in the hallway. Balding Christmas trees, stripped of tinsel, lie abandoned on the streets.

Christmas Crackers

The infantilism of the English is manifested in the Christmas Cracker. Of course in France we have our own *cotillons*, boxes of silliness for children's parties with clowns' hats and whistles and poppers.

But would we choose to decorate our tables with 'luxury crackers' containing pens, rings, or corkscrews or leather notepads? Crackers are pulled at the beginning of Christmas dinner so that all the guests can make themselves look hideous by putting on the paper hats. These will either split on big heads, or else slip down to mid-temple, flattening the hair. The crackers also contain weak jokes which are read out around the table.

Wrapping Presents

Unbelievably, the shops in England do not offer a gift-wrapping service. Or, if they do, you have to pay for it. So you spend all that money on presents, then have to buy paper and scotch tape and do it yourself. *Incroyable!* What a relief it is for me to get back to Paris and nod at the *vendeuse* in Bon Marché when she asks me, '*C'est pour offrir?*'

Sentimentality

As I hope I have made clear, the English are not given to expressing their feelings. Sometimes, when one is confronted by that phlegmatic demeanour, it is tempting to think it's because they don't have any.

This all changes at Christmas, when they sink into a sentimentality that has its roots in Charles Dickens and their Disney-esque friends across the Atlantic.

The shops are filled with schmaltzy 'chestnuts roasting by the fire' type songs by Bing Crosby, copies of *A Christmas Carol* and *'Twas the Night Before Christmas* make their way under the tree, as they dream of snowed-up houses thronged with those old-fashioned large families they forgot to have.

'Well, it's Christmas,' they say, shrugging off their usual stoicism to get dewy-eyed on the sofa in front of *It's a Wonderful Life* or *Oliver*. Strangers will nod and greet each other in the street. The man who delivers the milk may even get to claim his annual 'Christmas kiss'.

There is a downside to this, of course. Once the floodgates are open, resentment and depression comes hurtling in, as they measure up the reality of their own families against the pink-faced gracious lovingness of everyone else's. Suicides peak at Christmas in England, whereas in France, they are measured evenly throughout the year.

The Christmas Pantomime

'I will always remember the first English pantomime I saw, at the Théâtre des Variétés. It got a poor reception from the French, who considered the artists vulgar and mediocre; for my part, I was greatly struck by this manner of understanding comedy. . . a drunken riot of laughter, terrible and irresistible.' *Charles Baudelaire, On the Essence of Laughter*

It was with great curiosity and an open mind that I took the children along to see their first (and last) Christmas pantomime. As it was my daughter's birthday, I suggested she invite six friends along, to introduce them to this wonderful cornerstone of English cultural life. I knew Baudelaire had been a great admirer of *le grotesque anglais*, and I wanted them to experience, as he had, the *vertige de l'hyperbole**. Pantomime, he said, was the quintessence of comedy: pure, detached, concentrated.

Well, I'm not sure what pantomime he was talking about, but it certainly wasn't the production we saw of Aladdin and his amazing wonky lamp.

Advertised as 'fun for all the family', here was a coarse spectacle, littered with sexual innuendo and lame jokes, that my children informed me afterwards were based on characters from television shows. We know, of course, how the English rejoice in sexual confusion, but is there really anything funny about a big man dressing up as a grotesque 'dame' and

*Translator's note: 'vertigo of hyperbole': a characteristic French expression that manages to be both elegant and meaningless.

making jokes about flatulence? Can we honestly be expected to believe in a young woman dressed as a boy who falls in love with a girl? Must we be bullied into shouting 'Look out, he's behind you' every time the villain appears? I am glad to say my little French guests answered *Non* on all counts, and were as perplexed as I as to the purpose of the entertainment. *Franchement*, if we wanted to watch *les guignols*, we'd seek out the pier-end twenty-minute Punch and Judy show, never mind three tedious hours at the theatre. In addition, I felt obliged to apologize to the parents afterwards, for subjecting their children to this thoroughly debasing spectacle.

The Pantomime is yet another reminder that England is to France what Carthage was to Rome: debauched, bawdy, utterly without refinement. Why can't they enjoy proper mime instead, as perfected by ourselves? True, they occasionally put on Théâtre de la Complicité and Cirque du Soleil. And one sometimes sees gold-sprayed silent figures standing like statues in the street, which gives me a warm glow and makes me think of Paris. But in terms of 'entertainment' they just can't resist making fools of themselves in a show that lacks all discipline. The day I start to understand the appeal of the pantomime will be the day I return to France: for it will mean I have become English, and not merely French in England.

23

Socializing with the English

'Not only England but every Englishman is an island. He has all the qualities of a poker except its occasional warmth.'

Karl August von Hardenburg, Fragments

When I came to London, I was excited at the prospect of playing my own small part in furthering relations between our two great nations. With my links into the highest echelons of the banking fraternity, I would carry the torch for *La France*, and dazzle *les Anglais* on a more informal level with my *savoir vivre*.

In my foolish imagination – as I now see it! – I saw myself in an immaculate *petit tailleur* (my friend who is married to a diplomat had told me how important it is always to dress as an *ambassadrice* for French style), receiving all manner of Englishwomen to coffee around a pyramid of *petits gâteaux* which they would actually *eat*. Not to mention the *dîners en ville**, where cultural exchange would flourish.

Alas, I had misunderstood the insular nature of this island people. They may appear friendly, so refreshing and chatty on the surface, but in their own parlance, they 'keep themselves to themselves'. You can barely exchange a few words on the street, before they rush off, saying 'Don't let me keep you!' and I am barely exaggerating when I say that it is easier for a camel to pass through the eye of a needle than for a foreigner to be invited into an English home! How on earth was I to network? How could I hope to establish my own English version of *le piston*† with so few opportunities?

Once I had realized that my dream of making English friends was unrealistic, I revised my mission. Instead of suffering the humiliation of trying to befriend the natives, I would immerse myself in the French community in London. For here was a rich resource of wonderful people, and infinitely preferable to lonely days spent home alone, listening to Chérie FM on the internet. I have

---

*Translator's note: *le piston* is the system that drives good French society. It means knowing the right people, who all went to the best *grandes écoles* and are therefore best placed to pull strings.

never regretted this decision, and have even made some delightful English friends in the process, for where the heart of France beats, there too you find the very best type of English person, attracted like drab moths to the shining light of *la culture française.*

The French in London

Please do not think I am being London-centric when discussing the French community. I am merely being realistic. If we leave *l'hexagone*, it is *not* for the pleasure of hiding away in a provincial English town, but rather to take advantage of the work opportunities of the capital. If we wanted the provinces, we would have stayed at home, where we have twice the space for the same population, and a *paysage magnifique* which has not been turned into a giant carpark like southern England. But let me not digress in a nostalgic eulogy of the beauty of France!

In London, there are two sorts of French people.

1. *Cadres supérieurs**, who work in finance and oil:

---

*Translator's note: with French precision, workers are divided into *'cadre'* (executive) and *'non-cadre'* (non-executive).

très fréquentables* and such a relief to associate with people who share one's own values.

2. Young French people who cannot find work at home and who have come to learn English and work where they can. A study conducted by the London School of Economics pinpointed the city's attractions when it showed that the English capital is the only place in the world where you can arrive in the morning and have a job by the evening, and where people can earn a million pounds a year (though not, obviously, by that very evening). We would never tolerate such extravagant salaries, the social inequalities are *insupportable*, but France is France, GB is GB, and we all do as we can (though I must emphasize I am *cent per cent* opposed to Pierre-Marie's immoderate pay packet).

Where French People Live

'The French public does not like to be *dépaysé†*. They do not have very cosmopolitan tastes and are disturbed by new horizons.' *Charles Baudelaire*

*Translator's note: *fréquentable* is a wonderfully snobbish French term that means 'people worth knowing'.

I must disagree with Baudelaire who portrays us as unadventurous stay-at-homes. Just look at how we have adapted ourselves to London and made our very own enclave at South Kensington.

And it doesn't stop there! French people who cannot afford the Royal Borough have spread in all directions, though mostly to the west. The larger the family, the further they go. I know of at least two *comtes* and a *marquis* who have settled as far out as Ealing! Contrary to polite opinion in Paris, there is no shame here in living in the suburbs; indeed it can seem a sensible precaution when you consider the knife crime prevailing in the city centre.

Four Places to Meet French People

L'INSTITUT FRANÇAIS

A French cinema with a café where they serve Lu biscuits, proper *saucisson sec* and never a muffin or triangular sandwich in sight. They hold intellectual

†Translator's note: a neat term, literally meaning 'taken out of their country'. Widely used to refer to any kind of worrying change of territory. The French pay lip-service to the benefits of *dépaysement* for weekends and holidays, but you sense that beneath it all, they can't wait to get back home.

debates, wine tastings and the *fête de la musique* in June to mirror the Paris event. A lifeline.

L'AMBASSADE DE FRANCE

I usually delay my summer departure so as to attend the Bastille Day party at the Embassy. For me, it is a little foretaste of the refined summer pleasures that await me in the Luberon, with *canapés à la française*, and regional French wines, and evidence of French flair in novelties like meringues cooked in liquid nitrogen. Of course I realise that not everyone has my connections to secure an invitation, but there are many ordinary people present at this celebration of republican inclusiveness.

HYDE PARK

A great favourite with us, as it reminds us of the Bois de Boulogne. In the summer you will meet French families indulging in the local custom of the picnic. The Peter Pan playground is the only recreation for young children that comes close to the quality of those in the Jardin de Luxembourg, and you will hear many French voices.

SCOTLAND

We love the idea of Scotland, with its whisky, porridge and opportunity for wearing tartan shooting clothes. Take a mini-break there, as Pierre-Marie and I did, and you are bound to meet other French visitors with whom you can share your observations on the midges (like mosquitos but without the compensating warm weather), eccentric food (fat-sodden mutton pie or haggis followed by deep-fried Mars Bars) and climate, which makes England seem like the south of France in comparison.

How to Make English Friends

In spite of the rich social possibilities on offer from the French community, you may still feel you want to get to know the English. I have the following suggestions:

THE CATHOLIC CHURCH

If you are *croyant*, the church is a marvellous way to meet people. Catholics are a minority in England, and your *famille nombreuse* will be warmly welcomed. It is also useful to be Catholic if you have children as some of the best non-fee paying schools are only available to those of the faith, and you will have an *entrée* into a wide social spectrum (in contrast to France, where I am ashamed to admit the Catholic schools charge a token fee for the express purpose of keeping out the lower classes).

JOIN AN EVENING CLASS

Although you must never ask an English person *'Quelles sont vos passions**?'* (passion is regarded as deeply suspicious), they are very keen on 'hobbies' and evening classes to learn a new skill and meet people are very popular. Favourites include salsa classes (popular with the newly divorced), language classes (in order to deal with builders renovating their second home abroad) and counselling (most English people are retraining as counsellors of one type or another).

SHARE A FLAT

The best way for young people to make English friends is to enter into a *collocation,* which they call a 'flat share'. This is when you answer an advertisement to sleep in a house with strangers, which sounds like an extremely risky undertaking. I find it hard to understand the appeal of sharing a refrigerator and staring at other people's dirty *vaisselle,* yet many of my young compatriots have found it *très éducatif* to exchange the solitude of the *chambre de bonne* for such an experiment in communal living.

*Translator's note: it is embarrassing for us to be asked about our passions, but you must remember their over-inflated language is one of the things we love about the French.

JOIN THE RESIDENTS' ASSOCIATION

To see the English at their most emotional, go along to the meeting of your local residents' association. You will see the kind of passion we reserve for political meetings, as they become uncharacteristically heated on the subject of a new development or a traffic calming scheme. It is almost frightening to see the way they defend their *chez soi*, and if you can work up similar energy for parochial trivia, you will form a close bond with your neighbours.

Topics for English Conversation

To help you make friends with an English person, here are five opening remarks that will get the conversation flowing:

• 'Did you hear the one about. . .' Forget our scruples about telling jokes being *trop mec**. Funny stories related by either sex are always appreciated.

• 'Did you see the match?' Sport is always a safe topic, and generally silent men can become quite

---

*Translator's note: *trop mec* means 'too blokish', a frequent French complaint about English girls, especially the way they drink pints of beer, bellow with laughter, etc.

animated. You don't need any knowledge yourself, it will always be a monologue.

• 'Summer has been cancelled due to lack of interest!' A grim-faced acknowledgement of their terrible weather will always create a bond of sympathy.

• 'It's crazy isn't it, next door to me just went for a fortune.' Shaking your head about house prices will let an English person know you're one of them really.

• 'Cheer up, it may never happen!' The standard way to greet anyone who is not wearing an imbecilic smile.

English People to Avoid

Some types of *Anglais* are to be avoided at all costs. If you encounter any of the following, you must shrug in incomprehension and pretend you can't understand a word they are saying. That way they'll move on to another victim:

THE CHARITY MUGGER

Top of the list of undesirables, this is a would-be actor with a clipboard who will make eye contact at five metres and hold you hostage in the high street with his killer smile. The first time I was attacked, I pulled out a ten-pound note to buy my freedom, but this wasn't enough: he wanted me to sign a direct debit form there and then! In France, it would be considered an infringement of human rights, to be conned into sharing bank account details with a complete stranger.

Tip: At least they wear visible tabards advertising their charities, so you can take preventive action: though do take care in crossing the road – they usually hunt in packs and you're likely to run into his colleague.

THE STREET CRIMINAL

Even the smartest areas of London carry cheerful yellow boards advising residents of violent attacks that have just been committed in the locality. Street crime is rising, shootings and stabbings are not uncommon, in spite of bins helpfully provided by the police where thugs can go to dispose of their knives.

Tip: don't be a hero. If someone demands anyone your phone, your wallet, your iPod, just hand it over. In fact, if you think someone is looking at you in a threatening way, you could take pre-emptive action by offering them your handbag. Leave the foolish acts of courage to the Anglo-Saxons; remember, our strength has always been in clever negotiation.

THE CAR BORE

Many flashy cars are seen on the roads of this materialistic country, often in bright colours. Alas, their drivers are usually less vibrant. Excessive care is taken by all English people in parking, and should you inadvertently clip a bumper, all hell breaks loose. The car bore takes this pride in his machine to dreary extremes, and will expect you to admire him for owning it, and to enjoy listening to him talking about its technical capabilities.

The most popular man on television is Jeremy Clarkson, who drives cars very fast and makes sexist jokes. All Englishmen hero-worship him and wish they, too, had the courage to exceed the speed limit and cast off the shackles of political correctness inflicted by their American allies.

Tip: pretend you are a smug puritan who disapproves of cars.

THE FRANCOPHILE

One of the deadliest, he will speak at least some French, so you cannot pretend you don't understand. At a party he will make a beeline for you, and launch into a one-sided conversation about his house restoration in the Lot and the superiority of unpasteurized cheese. He will drive a French car, so there is some overlap with the car bore.

Tip: pretend you're German.

THE ANTI-AMERICAN

As a Frenchwoman, I am fully aware of the limitations of the Americans, but I don't need to make a religion of it. The anti-American bore self-righteously opposes US policies and culture in an indiscriminate way, and will use this blanket stance as a way of ingratiating himself with French people. He will indignantly recall the famous 'cheese eating surrender monkey' slur that was seized on by the British press, but which we treated with the disdain it deserved.

Tip: tell him you're half-American, that should shut him up.

THE GROOVY PARENT

A latter-day *baba cool* who goes to open-air rock concerts like Glastonbury and *takes her children*. Typically a middle-aged journalist who writes a feature about the experience and is photographed looking ridiculous swaying to the music *en famille*. It makes a nonsense of the British claim to be rock chicks of the world.

Tip: If someone suggests you book family tickets for a rock festival remember you're spending that weekend in France.

THE ALPHA CHRISTIAN

Someone who invites you to their house to hold hands and play guitar.

Tip: remind them that you are Catholic. So useful, even if you never go to mass.

THE UNEMPLOYED YOUNG PERSON SELLING DUSTERS

A disadvantage of houses opening on to the street (as opposed to an apartment block) is that you are a victim of door-to-door callers. Men drive down from Grimsby with vanloads of fish which they want you to buy in bulk for your freezer (though why I would want to pay extortionate fresh fish prices for food to freeze is beyond me).

24

Perfidious Albion

'In England we never entirely mean what we say, do we?
Do I mean that? Not entirely.
Alan Bennett, The Old Country

I wouldn't say the English were liars. I wouldn't even say they were 'economical with the truth', which is how they prefer to put it. But they will never say what they really think. Is it because they do not have an opinion? No! It is because (a) they hate confrontation, whereas we thrive on it, and (b) they have a pitiful desire to please, whereas we do not care whether people like us or not.

Let me give you some examples.

1. A friend has bought a house in France and is excitedly showing her friends the photographs. The English people will say, 'How wonderful! Lucky you, what a wonderful thing to do.' The French person will say, 'Do you have family in the area? Why did you buy a house there? It's too far, you'll never make proper use of it.'

2. A woman is proudly wearing a new dress that has cost her a lot of money. It does not suit her, it emphasizes the over-generous *rondeur* of her hips. The English friend says, 'It's gorgeous, the colour is perfect!' The Frenchwoman says, 'If you lost six kilos, it would look much better.'

3. Susan and Marie-Louise are on a visit to inspect the home improvements of mutual friends. Susan says, 'It's fabulous, you have done a fantastic job, you could not have done any better.' Marie-Louise says, 'Why did you not put a window in this wall instead of that one? The view would have been much better.'

Now, before you say those French people are being mean, and would do better to make kind remarks like the English, let me point out one thing. Everyone knows the 'mean' French person is right! She alone has had the courage to speak the truth! And the minute the victim has left the room, those 'kindly' English will all get the knives out and stab her in the back. 'Ridiculous place to buy a house!', 'Terrible dress!', 'Stupid to put the window there!', all delivered with a snort of treacherous laughter.

Perfidious Albion indeed!

How the English Say 'No'

The refusal of the English to speak honestly makes them almost impossible to understand, but I have learned a few tricks over the years. Here are some signs to warn you they are about to disagree violently with you – but without being 'nasty' about it.

THE KILLER SMILE

As practised by Tony Blair, it never means 'I agree with you'. It means 'I'm going to drop you in the *merde*, but go about it in a nice and friendly way.'

THE DOUBLE NEGATIVE

Can be made even more confusing through use of a fudging qualifier. 'I'm not a hundred percent sure I don't disagree with you.' 'I wouldn't necessarily say no'. 'You have to ask yourself if you wouldn't be better off not going down that road.' Don't waste time with the two-negatives-equals-a-positive calculation – believe me, it always means 'No'.

THE WAFFLING FILLER

'Don't get me wrong, I hear what you're saying.' 'Well, that's one way of looking at it,' None of these translates into French, our language is just too precise. What it means is 'I disagree with you but don't know how to say it.' Why can't they just say '*Non*'?

25

Multiculturalism

'We want British citizenship to embrace positively
the diversity of background, culture
and faiths that living in
Britain involves.'
David Blunkett, in the preface to Life in the United Kingdom:
A journey to Citizenship.

American philosopher Ralph Waldo Emerson
observed that while the English built London for
the English, the French built Paris for the whole
world.

How ironic that of the two cities, it is London that
has become the home city for so many foreigners!
For a country that prides itself on not having been
invaded since 1066, it is, in fact, suffering invasion on
a daily basis.

As one of those invaders, I am first to applaud the
rich cosmopolitanism of London. Every day I marvel
at the influences from other countries that bring in
some much-needed flavour. Where would English

cuisine be, for instance, without immigration? And I do not agree with that *méchant* who said that once the English were in the EU, they threw the key over the door to let in everyone else!

However, I must point out that there are some disadvantages to the carefree rough-and-tumble of English society, where they are committed to 'celebrating diversity'. In France, we tolerate diversity, but try to keep it under control.

The first thing you need to know is that all debate about multiculturalism is taboo. If you so much as hint at the idea that there might be drawbacks, you will be branded a *Le Pen-iste* and a crazed reader of the popular 'tabloid'* press.

Nevertheless, in the French spirit of passionately seeking out the truth, I must point out two aspects of *le multiculturalisme* that, in my opinion, might cause concern *outre-Manche*†.

Let Them Not Speak English

Whether we like it or not, English has become the leading language of the world, and everyone wants to

---

*Small format newspapers that I always find entertaining for their salacious stories, but are frowned upon by liberal *bienpensants* as sinister vehicles for right wing propaganda.

†Translator's note: the other side of the Channel.

speak it. Yet the authorities do everything they can to prevent immigrants from learning it!

I sometimes wonder why I bothered to take extra English lessons before I moved here. Information from the Mayor of London's office is available in fifty-seven languages, and if you manage to come up with a different tongue, they will oblige with an interpreter.

There would be a riot in France if the taxpayer had to pay for this service. Like Ancient Rome before her, France embraces all comers – on condition that they speak our glorious language. And we make sure our *fonctionnaires* are fierce enough to frighten off those who fail to comply. Bee enjoys recounting her eight-hour queue at the Préfecture to obtain her *carte de séjour*. When at last it came to her turn, she and her husband were sent to the back of the queue because they had only taken one queuing ticket between them, even though they had a shared dossier. She asked why they didn't put up a notice telling people they need one each? What's the point, said the charming *fonctionnaire*, most people in here can't read French.

I think the English could do with a little more of that attitude. You can't expect foreigners to speak the local language if you spoonfeed them. It would be like me coming to live in South Kensington and speaking only French. And I am ashamed to say that I *do* know people who have fallen into that very trap.

Positive Discrimination

In what can only be described as inverted prejudice, the English will always want to know the racial background of a job applicant, especially in the public sector.

I have an English friend who recently applied for a government post after a distinguished career in banking. During the interview, he sensed he was being looked down on as white and middle class, which was indeed revealed to be the case at the end, when one of the interviewers voiced concerns that he had not had much experience of minority groups. It was with great enjoyment, he said, that he was able to reveal to them that he was in fact gay, and therefore almost as deserving as a member of an ethnic minority.

A word of warning: if you live in London, be careful not to complain about what brave detractors call 'political correctness gone mad'. If you do, you'll be branded a fascist.

It makes one wistful for what we call '*la France du non*'.

26

English Manners

'The English are too busy, they don't have time to be polite.'

Montesquieu

My biggest shock on moving to England was discovering how rude the English can be. Where was the kindly bowler-hatted gentleman of my imagination who held open doors and said 'After you'? He had turned into an ill-mannered 'hoodie'.*

The only gentlemen left are on television, in nostalgic costume dramas, where old-fashioned decency is expressed through the visual medium of breeches and naval uniform.

Even the English are appalled by how rude they have become. Everywhere you look there are books and newspaper columns addressing the confusion of

---

*A young person who expresses his disaffection by wearing a sweatshirt with the hood up. The English have demonized these poor unfortunates by banning them from shopping malls.

modern manners. They highlight a shocking truth: the English no longer know what is correct behaviour. They have thrown out the old rule book, and failed to come up with a new one.

There are now just two cast-iron rules:

Don't be racist
Don't jump the queue

Apart from that, anything goes. And to think they berate us for being rude!

Let me give you some examples of rude English behaviour. In their defence, I would say one thing. A lot of their rudeness is not deliberate, but a manifestation of intense *embarrassment*. They have always been the most easily embarrassed people in the world; now things have reached crisis point as they ask themselves, 'How are we *supposed* to behave?' This is the pressing question underlying every other clumsy *faux pas*.

Avoidance of Eye Contact

Even before you've spoken to them, you know *les Anglais sont différents*, by the way they refuse to look you in the eye. What could be ruder than seeing me walk towards them, then turning away their gaze as if I did not exist? If you want to be kind, you can put it down to shyness or political correctness – remember you can be imprisoned here for admiring a woman. They call it harassment; we call it our *raison d'être*.

Failure to Extend a Correct Greeting

Gone are the days when an English person on meeting you would shake your hand and ask 'How do you do?' Nowadays, it's a nod and a limp 'Hello', which is a great pity: the handshake gave them something to do with their arms, which now hang uselessly by their sides.

Kissing

Social kissing has caught on, but is still considered a continental affectation. The English kiss but make a joke of it: 'Ooh, both cheeks!' Physical contact is abhorrent to them, so kissing on arrival is stiff and uneasy, and everyone is relieved when it's out of the way.

A note for my male readers: Englishmen never kiss each other, unless they are gay. I have seen an Englishman look on enviously as two Frenchmen embrace each other with warmth and machismo. You can tell he yearns to shed his inhibitions and throw his arms round his friend. But he is just too repressed.

Pierre-Marie finds it is always advantageous to kiss the hand of Englishwomen as they find it endearingly foreign. Chirac got into trouble with the British press at a summit when he kissed the hand of every other lady foreign minister, except the English minister Margaret Beckett, but I think he was just respecting the Anglo-Saxon pretence that women and men are indistinguishable.

Filer à l'anglaise

To avoid the embarrassment of saying goodbye, the English often just melt away, from which we draw our expression *filer a l'anglaise*. It is unthinkable for us to drift off like that without terminating the meeting with a proper sign-off, be it '*Au revoir Monsieur*' or a warm embrace.

'Thank you' and 'Sorry'

To make up for not having proper manners, the English say 'thank you' and 'sorry' all the time. We French are far too respectful of people to waste their time on such inanities. Why apologize without cause? And why say thank you five times when once is sufficient?

Yet French people are considered rude because we prefer not to keep up a constant gush of gratitude. When we say '*Merci*' it is sufficient. When the English say, 'Thanks, thank you, great, lovely, thank you, thanks, thanks,' it is just a meaningless babble.

As for the apologizing, that is downright confusing. If you inadvertently tread on their foot, they'll spin round to apologize, presumably for daring to have a foot at all. Worst of all is when the apology is the preface to a savagely rude outburst. As in 'I'm sorry, but that is the biggest load of b—ks I've ever heard. . .' To my mind, this is the epitome of bad manners: to *appear* to be apologizing, then to launch into a blistering personal attack. It is also entirely and typically English.

Being '*Correct*'

'It is wise to apply the oil of refined politeness to the mechanisms of friendship.' *Colette, The Pure and The Impure*

When confronting the rudeness of the English, you may run up against counter-accusations like this: 'The French are arrogant. They never smile, aren't helpful and get very impatient. They may say *Bonjour*

madame and all that but it's just a parody of politeness, underneath they're really rude.'

This shows how profoundly they have missed the
point. The purpose of good manners is to provide a
code of *correct* behaviour, regardless of what you
really think of the other person. Calling a customer
Madame is *correct*, but you can still let her know she
is a nuisance for not having the right change. Holding
the door open for the person behind you is *correct*,
but if they are walking too slowly, of course you
should scowl at them for making you wait. If
someone's jacket slips off the back of his chair, it is
correct to pick it up, but by all means warn them that
you won't do it again. Being polite does not mean
relinquishing the advantage.

Never forget that French used to be the international language of diplomacy, exquisite in its subtle
nuances and use of the subjunctive. Its replacement
by English is a tragedy. You still read echoes of that
elegance in the way we sign our letters, begging our
recipients to believe in the distinguished expression
of our most sincere devotions. The English prefer
to keep it short and squat. Cheers, Regards. Best.
All best.

Too busy to be polite, as Montesquieu reminds us.

Polite Conversation

The English have two odd ideas about being polite in conversation:

• Never Be Silent. They would rather talk nonsense than fall silent. How often have I heard English complaints about what they consider to be awkward silences around a French dinner table. We are intelligent enough to know that if one has nothing to say, then one says nothing. Whereas they will feel obliged to 'keep the conversation going', even if this means talking about the weather.

• Never Disagree. In French conversation, we enjoy taking a personal stand on a topic, and defending it with passion. In England, this is considered very bad manners. If you disagree, you keep your opinion to yourself, and nod along with the general consensus. This starts in childhood. My friend's daughter felt victimized at school, because she disagreed with her classmates about the merits of a particular singer. Instead of respecting her opinion, the other children would not rest until she had backed down and fallen in with their opinion. This mild bullying persists through adult life and suppresses debate in the name of polite behaviour.

They call this 'not being arrogant'. We call it weak-mindedness.

Response to Acts of politesse

The English are scared of being polite, as they never know how a well-meaning gesture will be received. A young man will sit engrossed in his newspaper on the tube, fearful of offering his seat to a woman. She might bite his head off, or just say 'No, you're all right,' making him feel foolish and old-fashioned. We have never gone in for that silly aggressive feminism that defends women's right to suffer like a man. Gallantry is a sweetener of daily life, but it is a pleasure the English prefer to forego.

An incident I witnessed on a bus illustrates the suspicion the English accord to acts of civility. I was accompanying a party of French children on the upper deck, when a man left his umbrella on his seat. A French boy picked it up and rushed to the stairs: 'Please sir, you've forgotten your umbrella.' The man gruffly thanked him, and the boy turned to his friends and said, in English, 'That's what kids are made for!' The children laughed, the boy sat down, but the man came storming back up the stairs, face like thunder, to threaten the boy: 'What did you say to me?' He had heard the laughter, and assumed the boy had been mocking him. I am glad to say I took him to task. Is it any surprise, I said, that your children are so appallingly behaved, when that is how you respond to an act of politeness?

Lack of civisme

Education civique lies at the heart of our education, but can you believe it plays no part in the English curriculum? So no surprises that the English become bad citizens, all jostling for personal gain with no thought for the common good, which is the basis of all *politesse*.

Our own excellent manners are based on *le respect d'autrui,* the respect for others. I have made it my personal mission to try to educate my English friends, to open their eyes to the civic gestures they could make in order to become more like us. Here are my suggestions:

INTRODUCE A WEALTH TAX/*IMPÔT SUR LA FORTUNE**.
There is no wealth tax in England, though so many people are rich. In France, we are proud to pay the ISF,

---

*Translator's note: ISF is a tax payable in France on any assets above the value of 740,000 euros.

as a gesture of solidarity. And if we happen to know that our neighbour has not paid, it is our civic duty to report them. It's not a question of denunciation, it's just being *correct*.

The English would call it 'snitching'. They fail to understand that suggesting a *contrôle fiscale* is a useful way of reminding your neighbour that he has fallen down in his duty of *fraternité*, for example by failing to lend you his lawnmower.

DON'T BE MEAN ABOUT PUBLIC PROJECTS
The *radin** Brits can't see the point of grand gestures, and would rather have a tax rebate. They should have let us host the Olympics; we wouldn't have made a fuss about the odd billion.

PRIORITY TO WOMEN WITH CHILDREN
Those in possession of a French *carte de famille nombreuse* are of course entitled to go straight to the front of a taxi queue. By offering similar rights, the English could learn some proper respect for young families which might prevent them from making such a huge fuss about something as commonplace as having a child.

---

*Translator's note: stingy. Only the Dutch are considered more *radin* than the British.

LEARN TO TURN A BLIND EYE

The English should show more imagination in legal affairs. Our own tradition whereby the *notaire* leaves the room during property transactions – allowing vendor and purchaser a moment together to conduct whatever private business they see fit – is both pragmatic and public spirited, and stories of suitcases of cash changing hands are wildly exaggerated.

MODERATION WITH OBSCENITIES

Elegant and expressive in our diction *à la francaise*, we do not go in for swearing. We reserve a small pool of colloquial vocabulary – *con, pute, merde* – which is occasionally dropped into conversation for emphasis, and that's as far as it goes.

In contrast, the English have a breathtaking store of obscenities that may be unleashed in a savage stream at any opportunity. My own good manners prevent me from listing the words, but at any moment you can expect to hear a violent outburst of guttural Anglo-Saxon sounds.

Football Fans

For all their posturing about peace and tree-hugging, the English pride themselves on being big, brave and violent: simple-minded giants built like Norse warriors, who jeer at us for being small, clever and Napoleonic.

With limited opportunities for warfare, this belli-cose Anglo-Saxon finds an outlet in one important area of British life: football. The football fan is prob-ably not a hooligan – they are the minority – but he will walk with a crude swagger, tossing his beer can and fish-and chip wrapper into people's gardens on his way to the match, where he sings humorous songs, like 'Hate Man United, we only hate Man United', 'Does she take it up the Arsenal', or 'You'll never walk again'*.

These chants are lovingly reported in books and newspapers as examples of English wit and fighting spirit.

Behaviour in Restaurants

I don't need to point out that there is good and bad noise to be found in restaurants. In France, you hear good noise: the animated buzz of enlightened conver-sation, the enthusiastic exchange of views of the menu.

In English restaurants you are deafened by braying, whooping, loud voices cracking jokes to someone at

---

*A play on the anthem 'You'll Never Walk Alone', alluding to the threat of violent attack from which the victim will never recover.

the other end of the table. This is also the noise they bring into our restaurants at home when they come visiting. To cope with this, the best Paris restaurants have allocated a separate area, a sort of social Siberia in an unfavoured upper room, say, where the English can shout without disturbing the other diners.

Alas, no inverse arrangement exists for French people dining in London! Even in the most expensive establishments, we must take our chances and risk being seated between parties of heavy drinking groups shrieking at each other and possibly even throwing food.

Oddly, in view of the low standards of adult behaviour in restaurants, children are not welcome. They are considered a bore, because they cannot join in the drunken revelry, and because they are not trained to sit for more than ten minutes at the table. Instead, they are taken to fast-food outlets, family rooms in pubs, and special 'child-friendly' restaurants like Blue Kangaroo where glum-faced fathers drink in appalled silence as their offspring run wild around them.

Intolerance of Smokers

Although I have given up smoking, I occasionally have recourse to *une Marlboro light* if I am feeling *un petit creux** and might otherwise be tempted to fall into bad English snacking habits. I see this as a small sacrifice to make in the interests of keeping my figure. Yet the English *bourgeoisie* display zero tolerance and will force you out into the garden. Since the ban on smoking in public places, they are no longer able to vilify people in restaurants, and private homes are the only places where they can express their disapproval. Only the working classes remain civilized in this respect.

My Conclusion: Let Them Look to France!

Scott Fitzgerald said that France has the only two things towards which we drift as we grow older – intelligence and good manners. I can only agree, and thank *le bon Dieu* that I was born French and therefore programmed to behave impeccably.

*Translator's note: literally 'a little hollow' or hunger pang.

27

Class: Let Me Crack the Code

'England is the most class-ridden country under the sun. It is a land of snobbery and privilege.'

George Orwell, England Your England, 1941.

The English are the most appalling snobs, who are always worrying about what 'class' they belong to.

This is utterly foreign to us, as we disbanded class divisions once and for all in 1789. For the record, however, I should just clarify that my family, the de Monplaisir, are *noblesse d'épée*, or what the English would call 'old money', as opposed to new money *noblesse de robe*.

Prime ministers John Major* and Tony Blair both told the nation that the class war was over when they pronounced 'We're all middle class now.' Nobody believed them.

*the one whom nobody remembers.

le Dossier

Class Snobbery: Interpreting the Signs

The English love to point out class difference, and are especially critical of those who fraudulently try to change the station they were born to. Here are some examples:

TALKING 'POSH'

Like all English snobs, Bee has an ear finely attuned to other people's accents. She has tried to educate me in this art, using Tony Blair's voice as a case study. Privately educated, he speaks in an upper-class 'public school accent'* also known as Received Pronunciation, but more widely described as 'posh'. This could pose a problem for the leader of the *travailliste* party. So when he addressed a trade union conference, or was speaking to factory workers, he would loosen his vowels, drop his aitches and introduce glottal stops in a subconscious bid to ingratiate himself with the 'common man'.

This is fascinating to us, as everyone in France speaks in the same way, except for regional accents, and we cannot guess the social origins of a person from the way he talks.

Bee tells me, with some regret, that the English talk

*Also known as the Queen's English.

a lot less 'posh' than they used to. If you listen to BBC archive footage from the Second World War, the tortured upper-class accents of the presenters are almost unintelligible. Only Prince Charles talks like that now. Whereas French broadcasters from the same period sound entirely contemporary. Even twenty years later, BBC girl reporters interviewing Bob Dylan spoke in artificial 'cut-glass' accents that quite belied their groovy 'dolly-bird' appearance. Today, the media go out of their way to have 'ordinary' voices. The only really posh voice in broadcasting belongs to a black man, Trevor McDonald.

Having a 'common' accent is no longer a bar to success. Gone are the days when an East End boy needed elocution lessons if he wanted to get on (my friends in fashion tell me this was the case for the managing director of an upmarket magazine group).

'Working Class Taste'

The English have an acutely tuned sensitivity to anything 'naff', which means working class. Furry dice hanging from the car mirror, shiny 'reproduction' furniture, porcelain miniatures or dolls in national dress arranged in alcoves, are all dismissed with a knowing snigger as 'naff' (formerly 'common', but that term is now outlawed).

This would be unacceptable in France, where nobody would sneer at someone else's décor. And anyway, even those of us *de bonne famille* buy repro furniture, since we prefer our homes to look new and clean, unlike the battered old antiques the English favour.

REVERENCE FOR TOFFS

However much the lower orders sneer at each other, all English people love a proper old aristocrat. They melt at the knees at the qualities they perceive as his prerogative – and of which they are deeply envious: his eccentricity, his determined philistinism, that dirty old waistcoat with egg stains and his complete disregard for personal appearance. It turns them into fawning courtiers on a Versailles scale.

Favourite aristocrats include politician Sir Anthony Wedgwood Benn, who gave up his title to become plain Tony Benn, and dear old 'Debo' Devonshire, the Duchess, from the eccentric Mitford family, who ran a house* with 50 bedrooms. Visitors to stately homes are always thrilled to have a sighting of the lord or lady of the manor, and like to discuss

*Her book about Chatsworth, *The House*, was a bestseller.

it afterwards, telling their friends how 'friendly' and 'natural' they were, just like ordinary people.

They would never have had the stomach for *la révolution*.

TELL-TALE VOCABULARY

To borrow an English expression, in France we like to call a spade a spade, or rather, *un canapé, c'est un canapé*. We don't have to worry if it is a sofa, a settee or a couch.

In England, there are tedious class-based alternatives for many everyday objects, first indicated by Nancy Mitford in her book on 'U and non U' (meaning Upper Class and non-Upper Class) which set the tone for modern English snobbery. This, presumably, is what the English are referring to when boasting about the richness of their vocabulary.

As a foreigner, you can rise above it and choose whichever word you like. But if you want to be posh, choose the Anglo-Saxon option over the French, which is likely to be aspirational lower-middle (you see how contagious it is, this decadent talk of class!). So, napkin instead of serviette, sorry not pardon. The following French words are not used in posh conversation, unless they are pronounced in a silly voice to show you are mocking the sort of people who habitually use them: billet doux, toilette, lingerie, bidet and ensuite (meaning bathroom).

'Transcending Class Barriers'

'I come from an ordinary background,' said a celebrated woman explorer in a recent interview, 'it was unthinkable for someone like me to go to the Arctic.'

Not so unthinkable, surely, in the modern world? But in England, you are still supposed to 'know your place'.

The appeal of Princess Diana's butler's ingratiating 'serve-and-tell' memoir is all about class: how incredible that 'someone like him' should become so intimate with the ruling classes. The English were fascinated by the daring trajectory of Paul Burrell, who dominated the newspapers for a month.

From Ladette to Lady, a television reality show, promised to turn chavvy girls into proper little gentlefolk. This would never work in France, where everyone knows how to behave correctly.

These stories are all about social position: not rags to riches stories, but lower class to upper class.

Upstairs, Downstairs

Rather as the English operate a two-tier system for feeding adults and children (effortful gourmet production for the first, frozen rubbish for the second), so they instinctively know that upper and lower classes have different tastes in food. Just so you know:

Lower middles must have 'builder's tea' (they don't like the fancy ones you keep for yourselves*), instant coffee instead of filter, white sliced bread, white sugar and processed food.

Of all the affronts to our French sense of democracy, this is the most shocking. Our great contribution to the world has been to establish the sacrosanct right of every man to eat like a king, or at least like a *bourgeois*.

*Personally, I still prefer to buy my tea in Paris, from Mariage Frères who used to supply the Russian Tsar. My current favourite is 'Fall in Love' black tea with rose petals.

TEN REASONS TO HATE THE ENGLISH

I have been at pains in this little guide *not* to sink to the cheap levels of xenophobia that the English display when they write about the French. You will appreciate my even-handed assessment of our dear neighbours, written without malice or prejudice.

However, there are things about the English that, if I'm honest, infuriate me beyond belief. And just for 'fun', as they would say, let me list them for you.

1. They never say what they think, yet pride themselves on their 'plain speaking'.

2. They change the way they talk according to who they are talking to: blokey when addressing their builder, then cold and posh on the phone to their bank.

3. Their false modesty. In reality, the English are viciously competitive.

4. They have too much money and buy up our country homes.

5. Their idiotic cheerfulness. Why can't they embrace the dark side, the way we do?

6. Their sinister failure to move their arms when they speak.

7. Their big bottoms.

8. Their leaden jokes about how drunk they were last night.

9. Infuriating forms of address (would you like anything else with that *at all*?, will you do that *for me*?).

10. Being very precise about uninteresting details, for instance the exact route taken to drive from one town to another.

MAIS QUAND MÊME. . .

TEN REASONS TO LOVE THE ENGLISH

1. They are open to new ideas.

2. Eccentricity. We must admit it is refreshing to see people dressed *n'importe comment*.

3. Freedom of speech. Imagine our politicians being subjected to such rude questions!

4. One can go shopping for clothes on Sunday.

5. The 24-hour supermarket. We hate the supermarkets of course, but they can be useful.

6. 'Happy-go-Lucky' (which does not translate into French). They don't care about correct form.

7. Le fair play!

8. Hyde Park.

9. Sense of humour. Wearisome, but 'fun' if you enter the spirit.

10. Their touching sense of pride in being English – in spite of everything!

LEXICON

Here is a list of commonly used English words and phrases that require more explanation than you will find in *Le Petit Robert*.

'Bless. . .'
Sentimental utterance intended to show generous spirit of person who says it, meaning 'How sweet. . .'

Bully
Unpleasant child who attacks his weaker classmates, physically and emotionally, and grows up to succeed in the workplace. There is no French translation.

Fag hag
Woman who enjoys close friendships with homosexual men.

'Have a good one'
Irritating way of wishing you a happy Christmas.

'Move on'

Useful justification for not feeling anything. Whereas we like to brood on painful emotions, the English will be encouraged to 'move on'.

Muffin top.

Tyre of flesh that hangs over a low-cut pair of trousers. Can be concealed by a 'clever top', but more effective when left fully exposed.

Quality time

The holy grail of every English person, which they hope to achieve by moving abroad for a new life with their family. Though why your unappetizing husband should become more desirable in a new setting, I don't know.

Sicky

'Throwing a sicky' means taking a day off work due to illness. As the English are never ill, throwing a sicky is always an act of dishonesty.

Sorry

Not only do the English apologize all the time, even when you bump into them, they will get aggressive if you don't do the same. When in doubt, say 'Sorry'. They like big public apologies too – most recently they were sorry for slavery, and we look forward to them saying sorry to us for giving us mad cow disease and buying up all our houses

Special

For us, *spécial* is a fat oyster or someone worthy of suspicion. For the English it means educationally challenged, as in 'special needs', or a sentimental form of approbation: 'I wanted to do something really special', 'You're special', 'I'm special', etc.

Wedgy

Only the English could come up with a word to describe the portion of the underpants that becomes trapped between the buttocks when sitting down. Even girls will claim to have one, though 'Ooh, I've got a wedgy,' does little to enhance their charm.

AFTERWORD: VIVE LA DIFFÉRENCE!

Last summer, at the Bastille Day celebrations at the French Embassy in London, my dear friend the Ambassador made a moving address to the assembled guests. We were a vibrant, eclectic party of business people, artists, artisans, academics, civil servants, restaurateurs, movers and shakers from both sides of the Channel.

'*Chers amis*,' he said, 'you may think we are constantly opposed, but it's not true! We just make different choices.' He then reminded us that *La France est forte*, and led an emotional rendition of La Marseillaise, which always brings tears to my eyes, and as I sang I was struck by the sight of his wife singing by his side, slim with good ankles in a perfect cream suit.

Touched by his words, I looked around the garden and thought how those different choices were not restricted to honest, republican values versus decaying old monarchy. There was also the choice of whether to look after oneself, and dress well in *tenue de ville*, or whether to have a big stomach and shoes that don't match your outfit. Whether to look dashing in a well-cut suit and shiny, pointed shoes, or whether to wear a stained cricket tie and scuffed loafers. Whether to accept a single glass and one or two *amuse-bouches* or whether to crowd round the champagne bar, stuffing oneself with *canapés*.

In short, whether to be French, or whether to be English.

And then I thought, Why choose? I am French, yet I adore the English. My clothes are French, but, as Saki once said, I 'wear them with an English accent'. I respect French eating habits, but still make room for the odd binge on fish and chips! Truly, I am a product of the Anglo French alliance, as bi-cultural as the Channel Tunnel.

I hope this book has brought you some illumination. I hope that I have succeeded in showing you the English not as the odd barbarians you once thought, but a well-meaning people, whose eccentricities offer a valuable counterbalance to our own fine intelligence. They have their humour, and we have our *savoir vivre*.

Vive l'entente cordiale!

Your very own
Hortense de Monplaisir